west coast
coast
rooms

ROCKPORT

First published in the United States of America by
Rockport Publishers, Inc.
33 Commercial Street
Gloucester, Massachusetts 01930-5089
Telephone: (978) 282-9590
Facsimile: (978) 283-2742
www.rockpub.com

ISBN 1-56496-816-2

10 9 8 7 6 5 4 3 2 1

Design: Walter Zekanoski
Cover image: Malibu Residence, Kanner Architects; Photo by Tom Bonner.

Printed in China.

west coast

Portfolios of 41
Architects and
Interior Designers

coast

rooms

EDIE COHEN

GLOUCESTER MASSACHUSETTS

ROCKPORT
PUBLISHERS

contents

In 1977, I moved from London to Los Angeles. My artist wife, Annie Kelly, and I both needed new horizons. At the time, LA seemed so remote to some of my English friends that it was like going to the moon. It would certainly have been more logical, career-wise, to have relocated in Paris, Milan, or New York—all international media centers for the design industry at that time.

Nonetheless, what we both loved about LA was its exotic visual environment. In London, I never walked around with a camera. During my early LA years, I was never without one, constantly cruising the city and its surroundings, including Palm Springs, documenting the uniquely graphic buildings and landscapes suffused with visual ironies, and all lit by a brilliant desert sun.

Another seductive attraction of LA was the superiority of its lifestyle over that of other major cities. Here you could seemingly have it all: a house surrounded by a garden, right in the middle of town, and a climate suited to indoor-outdoor living.

In no time we had a house in the hills, behind the Hollywood Bowl, with two tiny gardens—cactus in front, and tropical at the back—with a variety of trees providing a year-round supply of fruit: loquats, figs, oranges, avocados, and bananas. French doors opened to admit the fragrance of roses and jasmine. All for the price of a small apartment in New York.

LA is, of course, the quintessential twentieth-century city. With overlays of 1950s and 1960s architecture, it was also the ultimate mid-century modernist city, one which composed itself into a David Hockney painting wherever you looked, where stuccoed buildings and iconic palm trees formed inevitable graphic statements. Into this blissful landscape, we inserted ourselves with our early 1960s Cadillacs, their trunks filled with Eames and Noguchi furniture from thrift stores.

Besides these indulgences, I had been attracted to this city for another reason. It was easy in the 1970s to dismiss LA as a cultural wasteland, but I had already met enough Angelenos to know that there was the promise here of something edgy and different. One of these was the artist Ed Ruscha, whose work was filled with a laconic humor that I had never encountered before. Also, there was the little-known architect Frank Gehry, whose studio I used to visit and whose work I began to document, something no on else was doing at the time. Some of these projects—the Davis house included—I took to show Mildred Schmertz, senior editor of *Architectural Record,* in New York. She was affectionately dismissive (and prophetic!): "Dear Frank, one day I'm sure we'll find a way to publish him."

As I write this, LA (and California) is greatly changed from the early days. We respect the memory of the early pioneers—Rudolf Schindler, Frank Lloyd Wright, Richard Neutra, and others—who in the 1920s invented the indoor-outdoor lifestyles that we now take for granted. I am reminded about the relative richness of our Californian lives, when I read the admittedly ironic assertion by New York writer, Fran Lebowitz, that "the outdoors is what you must pass through in order to get from your apartment to a taxicab."

West Coast Rooms celebrates the vast variety of permutations and solutions that its ever-ingenious designers and architects have adopted to render the maximum benefit from our wonderful climate, whether in LA or outside it.

Photo: Tim Street-Porter

Design: Thomas M. Beeton

introduction
by edie cohen

There is no such thing as West Coast design. Nor is there any such thing as West Coast architecture. Each design and architecture project is essentially a problem-solving exercise. As such, each responds to the program particulars of site, climate, budget, client tastes, and needs. To typecast West Coast design with generalities would not only be ludicrous, but also demeaning to an incredibly talented and daring group of professionals.

That said, designers and architects practicing on the West Coast do share in a passion for light and views. Daylight is the single most sought-after factor in every project—whether it be the white hot sunlight of southern California, the grayed, misty glow characteristic of San Francisco and the Bay Area, or the gray/green tinge of light illuminating Seattle and the Pacific Northwest. I, too, fell under its intoxicating spell. As an East Coast transplant, I discovered that waking up to sunshine meant that my day had a 50 percent guarantee of going well. As I became more deeply entrenched in the Los Angeles landscape, I learned how the

simplest of spaces possess certain richness when infused with daylight and a view facing the ocean or bay, palm trees, mountains or woods. Compared with all this, interior stuff—even the most cutting-edge design—pales.

True, the West Coast lacks some of the best aspects of East Coast living. We don't have the history and its corresponding architectural assets. Our grand old houses date only to the 1920s, and we certainly have no counterpart to New York's glorious prewar apartments rich with detailing and a patina of age. Nor do we have much of that other East Coast phenomenon that has come to be the preferred mode of urban living. Residential lofts, with their seductive invitations to design experimentation, are scarce on the West Coast. But, as part of life's grand compromises, climatic conditions here beg for indoor/outdoor living. Entire design schemes often begin with a courtyard or patio created to expand a house's square footage. Interestingly, this indoor/outdoor link also figures into commercial design where circulation corridors weave in and out of buildings.

In a sense, design in West Coast cities is more visually accessible. On the East Coast, much design is concealed behind formidable facades of apartment buildings or skyscrapers. I view the West Coast as more open, less anonymous. In Los Angeles, masterpieces by Frank Lloyd Wright, Rudolph Schindler, Richard Neutra, John Lautner, and Frank Gehry are only a car ride away. Gehry's own house in Santa Monica is only blocks from the local elementary school. Ask any kid who goes there; he'll be able to direct you to the master's constructivist bungalow. On view to all, design and architecture inevitably lead to an incurable condition. I call it house lust.

I present a portfolio of work by forty-one of the West Coast's design and architecture firms. Well established, many are familiar names to those who read the professions' publications. Others, however, are young with only a project or two to their credit. Through the work of both camps you can discover the diversity and the talent that constitutes West Coast design.

barbara
barry

Barbara Barry's interiors are analogous to today's glamour girls, connoting elegance, understated luxury, and a spirit of effortless grace. Her interiors tend toward a neutral palette and natural materials. The objects in her three-dimensional compositions are often equally weighted within a room. The fact that no one piece is overbearing leads to the serene atmosphere that has become an intangible trademark.

Barry was raised in a family of painters and studied at the Academy of Art in San Francisco. However, she considers herself self-taught. "Life has provided the most profound teaching. My mother was a vibrant mentor. When I traveled to Europe I felt the resonance of the arts and the layering of centuries of human acts done with elegance and celebration." She founded her Los Angeles-based practice in 1985.

Barry adheres to a modern sensibility, but draws from other design styles as well. Best known for her residential interiors, she also does commercial work with shops and restaurants to her credit. Barry is a vital force in product design and has executed furniture, lighting, fabric, and carpet collections. Be the project a product or interior, Barry holds the same considerations sacrosanct. "Line, scale, and proportion continue to be the essence of my design philosophy and practice," she says. "Design is a spiritual and tangible teacher. Design invites you to celebrate life."

In contrast to the steel, glass, and limestone of public spaces in a Balboa Island residence, the master bedroom is a study in sycamore, with the wood used for panaling, bed and side table. The bottom portion of sliding glass doors is sandblasted, while the transparent upper section provides a stunning beach and ocean view. Photo: Tim Street-Porter

"Nowhere is there light like at the beach," says Barry of a residence on Balboa Peninsula. The colors of the limestone, slip covers, and sycamore table take their tones from the colors of sand. "The hierarchy here is beach, architecture, then decoration." Photo: Tim Street-Porter

thomas m. beeton

"Design is like couture. It's always highly individual and appropriate. There's not much of a theme to my work." Yet Thomas Beeton's rooms do share common traits. Each space—be it traditional or contemporary—is consistently elegant in expression, understated in tone. Architectural detailing is honest and sincere. Furnishings, like the couture to which he alludes, are of the utmost quality but not necessarily precious. Beeton, who earned a degree in art history from George Washington University, had early professional training at Lord & Taylor, New York, and then opened an antiques shop in Los Angeles, embraces an all-encompassing design aesthetic. His rooms are always about "the mix." Fine antiques, contemporary pieces, and singular accessories create three-dimensional compositions with lasting appeal. "No matter the scale of the project," says Beeton, "my approach is always the same: to make the interiors suit the clients' needs in the hope that the rooms will feel upon completion as if they had always been there. I want to take the best of the clients' taste, collections, and way of life and make the design even better."

With his emphasis on clients' needs and preferences, Beeton calls himself an "undecorator." His rooms, by design, seem to represent a lifetime of collecting. Similarly, large-scale renovation projects often appear to have been built in an earlier era, belying the designer's intervention. The illustrated Brander residence is an example. No Mediterranean villa from the 1940s, this house, prior to Beeton's work, was a typical spec structure from the 1960s. It took Beeton's attention to scale, detail, romantic lighting, and care in assembling the elements themselves to effect the transformation.

Beeton elaborates on his design philosophy with succinct tenets. He avoids small, dainty gestures. Unflattering colors are a universal taboo, despite their in-vogue status. On an intangible note, he strives for qualities of abstraction and intuitiveness. "Un-decorating, de-designing and natural observance above all else," he says, "is the best design direction for any project."

(left) Furnishing icons by George Nelson, Christian Liagre, and Mario Bellini meet in a Brentwood, California, residence.

(opposite) Antique accessories—a pair of fluted columns, a Japanese scroll, and an Asian screen—add character to a classically furnished room. Photos: Tim Street-Porter

(above) The Branders' master bedroom was built to refer to Paris in the 1930s, yet be practical for today. Added columns enhance the arched structure of the room's entrance. "The architectural rigor plays well with the sexy shape and depth of the amboyna wood cabinet and the soft, voluptuous upholstery," says the designer.

(opposite) Renovated to resemble a gracious Mediterranean villa, the Brander residence in Brentwood has its interconnected living room and study filled with daylight. "The fireplace," Beeton comments, "is the centerpiece of the house and of the design direction—warm stone, great scale, and simple lines. I love taking cues from the architectural structure of every project—never smothering with fuss or unnecessary decoration." Photos: Tim Street-Porter

(above) For Beeton, the bedroom "should be the most sensational and inspirational of all. It is the one room you would always see last in the evening and first thing each morning." What better illustration than his guest bedroom with upholstered bed, vintage club chair, and antique rug.

(opposite) Thomas Beeton now. The living room of his Hollywood bungalow celebrates "the exuberance of the mix and the joy of the hunt." A large suede hide covers a vintage flea-market settee, which faces Paul Frankl's amorphous wood and cork table. The room is clearly sexy. Says Beeton: "The large chaise for two tries to imply comfort and possibly romance." Photos: Dominique Vorillon

hagy
belzberg

Despite his youth, Hagy Belzberg is already an award-winning architect with an impressive project roster. Since receiving his masters of architecture degree with distinction from Harvard University in 1991, he has received a Distinguished Building Design Award from the American Institute of Architects in 1998. He has completed restaurants, retail installations, galleries, and executive offices as well as private residences.

An architect with a finely honed design sense as well as knowledge of systems, engineering, and construction, Belzberg and his team make their projects eminently buildable as well as striking contemporary visual statements. One is impressed by wide-open interior spaces that extend, where possible, past the building's physical barriers to the exterior beyond. Ceilings tend to be high and distinctively expressed, either through form or material. The solidity of built environments is consistently offset by the transparency of glass expanses framing selected views. Given the southern California setting, where most of his homes are built, Belzberg's approach is particularly appropriate.

(left) A glassed-in corner backs a classic Eames rocker in the master bedroom of a Pasadena residence. Photo: Tim Street-Porter

(opposite) From an interior viewpoint, Belzberg's previous residence in Laurel Canyon, California, might well be considered a loft with function areas defined only by level change and object placement. Photo: Art Gray

For a residence built into a Pasadena, California, hillside, Belzberg's living space is a double-height volume enjoying seamless integration with a concrete-walled terrace. Photos: Tim Street-Porter

brayton & hughes

The residential interiors of Brayton & Hughes Design Studio tend towards interior architecture, as exemplified by the illustrated live/work loft at the base of the San Francisco Bay Bridge. Be the work a small interior design project or a large building commission, the design adheres to the same tenets. "Our approach is to bring to each new design a unique set of solutions appropriate to the individual requirements and geographical location of the project," comment partners Richard Brayton and Sanford Hughes. "Underlying the individual character of each project is a common foundation of exacting detail and carefully crafted richness of materials that derives from the architectural background of our key personnel." On a more tangible level, they add, "project management and cost control are essential elements of the design process."

Brayton & Hughes Design Studio was founded in 1989 by partners Brayton and Hughes, who were later joined by Jay Boothe. Since inception, the firm has completed an impressive roster of architecture and interior design projects throughout the United States, the Pacific Rim, Europe, and the Middle East. While known primarily for its commercial work, which focuses on hospitality and corporate installations, Brayton & Hughes accepts select residential commissions.

Brayton, Hughes, and Boothe were all associated with acclaimed leaders in the architecture and design fields, previously. Richard Brayton was design partner with Charles Pfister; Sanford Hughes was director of interiors at Skidmore, Owings & Merrill, San Francisco; Jay Boothe was a partner of Gruen Associates. Together, they hold more than sixty years of professional experience.

(left) A rolling stainless-steel ladder provides access to aluminum file boxes within a maple storage structure.

(opposite) Focal point of a 1,500-square-foot (135-square meter) live/work space is a double-height room serving as an office/meeting space and file archive. The table desk slides into the work wall cabinetry.
Photos: John Sutton

(above) Upholstered seating, set beneath an antique French advertising poster, defines the living or meeting zone. A hinged wall, which rolls on an inlaid metal track, conceals the kitchen. Upstairs are bedrooms and baths.

(opposite) The concrete and galvanized steel of the kitchen complement the refined industrial quality of the loft. A glass counter is built into the curved wall. Photos: John Sutton

Barry Brukoff concentrates on high-end residential design with modernist leanings, as do countless of his peers. Brukoff, however, distinguishes himself in several ways. Most of his commissions stem from the recommendation of the project's architect, initiating a collaborative process that starts during planning stages and carries through to completion. His status as a certified lighting designer brings another dimension to his work; lighting is an integral architectural component, not an applied afterthought. But perhaps what is most intriguing about Brukoff is his second career. He is an accomplished fine arts photographer, and his recently published book, Greece: Land of Light, is so titled because, he says, "of my interest in, and desire to capture on film, what light is capable of doing."

Years ago, Brukoff also pursued careers as a painter and sculptor. These endeavors continue to influence his work today. His interiors are consistent in their sculptural appreciation of space and form; they are characteristically rich in materials and color. And, his projects are filled with custom pieces and cabinetry illustrative of his hands-on approach. All this has roots in Brukoff's ties to the arts.

On a pragmatic note, the designer notes that his experience with large-scale government, commercial, and hospitality installations has made him an astute businessman sensitive to economic nuances. Budgets—established with clients at the onset—are meant to be adhered to, not broken.

(left) Richly colored canted planes and a slate staircase create an artistic entry to a San Francisco residence. Photo: Alan Weintraub

(opposite) In a 7,900-square-foot (711-square-meter) house in northern California, the double-height entry is dominated by a zinc bridge leading to private zones. The wood and zinc console is a custom piece. The Steinberg Group collaborated as architects. Photo: Barry Brukoff

(left) A mezzanine study, with views from its Oakland hillside site to the San Francisco Bay, sits below a bow-curved ceiling articulated with wooden beams. Brukoff collaborated with architect Ron Kappe in building the 4,500-square-foot (405-square-meter) house.

(below) In the Oakland hills residence, a classically modern dining room is separated from the kitchen by a cherry cabinet divider. Photos. Darry Brukoff

Firmly entrenched in the Los Angeles landscape, Carmen Nordsten Igonda Design (CNI Design) represents the partnership of two female architects with broad-based international backgrounds. Clara Igonda, a native of Argentina and graduate of the University of Cuyo with advanced degrees, spent years exploring the cultures and built environments of North and South America and Europe before settling in California. Her interests are as varied as her background. Prior to founding CNI Design, she was associated with several large architecture firms and participated in Los Angeles' vital art scene through corporate consulting and planning gallery exhibits. She also did a stint in the fashion world, creating exotic clothing that was sold in such high-style shops as Neiman Marcus and Saks Fifth Avenue.

Born in England and trained as an architect and interior designer in London, Josephine Carmen also worked with large architecture firms—in New York, San Francisco, and Seattle—before returning to Europe. First she collaborated on Paris' high-tech icon: Richard Rodgers' and Renzo Piano's Pompidou Center. Then it was back to London and a concentration on hospitality design, which eventually led to extensive work in the Middle East. As a result, Carmen became an avid student of Arab and Islamic cultures.

Despite diverse backgrounds, Carmen and Igonda share a design vision with roots in the International Style. Since starting their firm in 1988, they have completed retail, health care, hospitality, corporate, and residential interiors. "Our design," they say, "is based on modernist principals, utilizing materials for their intrinsic value." Norman Foster, Renzo Piano, Richard Meier, Tadao Ando, and Yoshio Tamaguchi count among their heroes. "We aspire," the partners state, "to emulate their clarity of design coupled with the poetic quality of beautiful materials and color."

(left) Similar to a pavilion in its relationship to its surroundings, the dining room has a table from Dakota Jackson and chairs from Donghia.

(opposite) A Los Angeles house designed by architect Robert Quigley evokes sensibilities of Rudolph Schindler and Frank Lloyd Wright. CNI's interior furnishings from Donghia, Dakota Jackson, and Todd Hase offer a luxurious counterpoint to strong construction materials. Photos: Toshi Yoshimi

james cutler

James Cutler earned a master's degree in architecture at the University of Pennsylvania where he discovered Louis Kahn as a kindred spirit. Leaving Penn for the Pacific Northwest, he engaged in architecture that celebrates the natural world and environmental correctness far before it became fashionable to do so. To quote James Wines in the introduction to Cutler's monograph: "James Cutler is one of those rare contemporary architects who has converted environmental technology, an ecologically responsible choice of materials, and a strong earth consciousness into art." Cutler's buildings bear strong relationship to site. The architecture becomes part of the environment without infringing upon it.

Clearly, Cutler's houses, with their celebration of natural materials and the emphasis on building systems that are visible within each structure, have a certain consistency. The illustrated Paulk and Wood residences and the Virginia Merrill Bloedel Education Center, which originates as a man's memorial to his wife and will eventually be used as a lecture hall, illustrate that. Yet within this vocabulary Cutler does not subscribe to a particular set of forms or standard solutions. Each project is its own unique investigation, adhering, above all, to Cutler's belief that architecture holds a responsibility to nature. Cofounding the Bainbridge Island Land Trust in 1988, he is responsible for the organization's acquisition of 1,000 acres of wildlife habitat.

(left) The Wood residence, placed between forest and meadow in Vaschon Island, Washington, is conceived as a private "night box" and public "day box," augmented by laundry and mud room, green house, garage, and horse barn. The detailed construction is designed to reveal every piece of wood used.

(opposite) Located on a waterfront bluff in Seabeck, Washington, the Paulk house has a view of the Olympic Mountains from its wooded site. The ceiling in the entry foyer is pulled back to reveal a strong sense of construction that is characteristic of Cutler's work. Photos: Art Grice

A 1,400-square-foot (126-square-meter) building of stone and timber post-and-beam construction on Bainbridge Island, Washington, is built as a memorial to the owner's sixty-two years of marriage. The house, which is on-axis with the wife's gravesite, will eventually be converted to a lecture hall. Photos: Art Grice

He's been called the master of minimalism. Yet minimalism in the hands of Orlando Diaz-Azcuy takes on its own meaning. It's far from stark and it's far from raw or brutal. As interpreted by the Cuban-born designer who emigrated to the U.S. in 1962, the aesthetic is infused with a richness of texture and perfectly selected objects that span time and stylistic ranges from antique to contemporary, super-sleek to baroque. "I like to simplify a room's design so you can look at things and appreciate what's there," he says. "But there's always room for baroque flamboyance." And, he adds, "one can appreciate the past and also be contemporary."

While best known for his spare and stunning interiors in both residential and commercial arenas, Diaz-Azcuy has a multidisciplinary background. He graduated from the University of California, Berkeley, with a master's degree in landscape architecture and city and regional planning. His own practice, founded in 1987 following twelve years as design principal for Gensler and Associates, Architects, includes architecture, landscape architecture, and a range of product design.

Design, for Diaz-Azcuy, is about process, not the end result. It is also about intuition and logic. "For a project to have a soul, your intuition has to be in it," he says. Residential work must reflect the client. Does he want luxury; does he seek status; does he want comfort? The illustrated Jacobs-Lee house, both built and designed by Diaz-Azcuy's firm, is a four-level townhouse created to accommodate a young professional couple's collection of African art accumulated during their travels on the continent. The straightforward building, with a continuous wall of hand-rubbed plaster and strategically placed niches throughout, provides a strong structural envelope for a range of possessions that include classic modern furnishings in addition to native art and artifacts.

(left) View of stairway landing towards the street shows hand-rubbed, terra-cotta colored plaster wall and oak flooring.

(opposite) Punctures in the four-story, rectangular volume on San Francisco's Telegraph Hill allow views through the house, whose credits are shared by Nestor Matthews of Mathews Studio plus Greg Stewart and David Oldroyd of ODA Design. Photos: Matthew Millman

(above) With Barcelona chairs, an antique console, and rattan table designed by Diaz-Azcuy, the living room adjoins the dining room, where niches for art top a storage wall.

(opposite, top) Diaz-Azcuy continued his antique/modern mix in the dining room with Saarinen's table and chairs complemented by an Asian chest. The end wall has a full-height inset of frosted glass.

(opposite, bottom) An ornate Chinese screen lends a quality of luxury to the otherwise spare master bedroom. Photos: Matthew Millman

Considered by many the mark of true luxury, the library has built-in shelving as a backdrop to Asian antiques, Florence Knoll seating, and **Mies' Barcelona table.** Photo: Matthew Millman

mark dziewulski

Essentially a modernist, Mark Dziewulski's approach to architecture is as rooted in culture and anthropology as it is in form, systems, and the aesthetics of design. He is passionate about architecture's role in both public and private arenas. "Good buildings express the dreams and desires of the people who live in them," he says. "Design should express the optimism that is characteristic of a healthy society."

Being a modernist for Dziewulski also means being attuned to the warp speed of technology and the immeasurable ways it continues to alter our lives. The architect, he attests, has a responsibility to respond to the increasing social isolation created by such phenomena as the Internet, telecommuting, and on-line shopping. Creation of stimulating settings for social and public life within the urban landscape is part of the solution. At home, corresponding influences result in environments with increasingly overlapping functions. Traditional rooms—one for each function—are rapidly becoming archaic. Increasingly, open spaces or the loft paradigm are becoming the sought ideal.

London-born and Cambridge-educated, Dziewulski came to the U.S. as the recipient of two consecutive Fulbright scholarships. He earned advanced degrees at Princeton, then worked with Michael Graves and Skidmore, Owings & Merrill before establishing an independent practice with offices in Sacramento and London.

A stunning, freestanding addition to a typical California ranch structure, Dziewulski's 1,200-square-foot (108-square-meter) pavilion translates much of his thinking into reality. Designed as a multifunction space addressing gallery, office, and lavish entertaining needs, the work stands as a dramatic piece of sculpture cantilevered over a manmade lake and surrounded by lush gardens. It follows in the tradition of California modernism. Through articulated glass elevations, which transform the project from a monolithic glazed block, Dziewulski not only minimizes barriers between built and natural worlds, but also capitalizes on sunlight while carefully manipulating views.

(left) Close-up view of the louvers illustrates alternating panes of transparent and translucent glass.

(opposite) The east elevation consists of glass louvers that not only provide a dramatic backdrop for sculpture, but also direct views away from the main house to the American River flowing at the edge of the property. Pomele cabinetry spanning the opposite wall is elaborately fitted for office storage. Photos: Keith Cronin Photography

In response to Sacramento's intense heat, the pavilion's west wall is conceived as a solid composition of overlapping planes—one limestone clad, the other plaster finished. The oculus within the roof overhang allows a circle of sunlight to travel through the interior during daylight hours. Photos: Keith Cronin Photography

(above) At the threshold of the glass-fronted building, a panel of etched glass embedded in the limestone flooring allows views to the lake. Three skylights, addressing the play of natural light, bring sunlight deep into the interior. The etched-glass desktop echoes the pavilion's scimitar form.

(opposite) A proponent of clean interior spaces, Dziewulski limits furnishings to a few classic chairs: the Eames lounge, Tom Dixon's S model for Cappellini, plus Jacobsen and Aeron seating. Photos: Keith Cronin Photography

One of Los Angeles' most prolific architects, Steven Ehrlich brings a unique background to his professional work. Upon graduating with honors from Rensselaer Polytechnic Institute, he spent six years in Africa. His first two years were with the Peace Corps, where he was among the first group of architects sent to Morocco. He then spent four years traveling, teaching, and studying the indigenous architecture of North and West Africa. His experience as what he calls "an architectural anthropologist" influenced his decision to settle in Los Angeles and continues to affect his work today.

"These experiences," he comments, "lead to an architecture concerned with vernacular response to climate and culture, the festivities of spontaneous social gatherings, and the power of simple forms and spaces." His projects, therefore, emphasize the interior/exterior connection that is a bonus of the southern California experience. They also engage the human component. "My artistic ideal," says Ehrlich, "is a quest that continues to put man in touch with nature, himself, and others in a spirit of excitement."

Ehrlich, who designs commercial, educational, and civic projects as well as residences, seeks to strengthen the connection between art and architecture. He has collaborated with several acclaimed artists and has been an advisor to the California Arts Council and served on the board of directors of a local museum.

(left) The 16-foot-wide (4.8-meter-wide) pavilion has three walls of glass and sliding-glass pocket doors to fuse interior and exterior.

(opposite) A 3,400-square-foot (306-square-meter) addition to a 1938 Neutra house overlooking the Pacific Ocean in Santa Monica joins a new entertainment pavilion, garage, and housekeepers' quarters with both the existing structure and the outdoors. Photos: John Edward Linden

(above) Ocher and burnt sienna tones of the Hempstead house in Venice allude to Ehrlich's African experience.

(opposite) Extensive windows and skylights flood the Hempstead house with light. Photos: Grey Crawford

Ronald Frink embraces the modernist tenets he defines as "clarity and integrity of building systems and forms." Yet he embellishes the definition. "The contemporary challenges that we have as designers is to draw upon those design basics and apply more adventurous colors and materials, and to more successfully address the need for creature comfort." He also strives to balance man-made forms with nature, never losing sight of the importance of landscape design and daylight as it affects both interiors and exteriors.

Academically and professionally, Frink is trained as a modernist. Completing undergraduate and graduate studies at the University of Illinois at Urbana and University of California at Los Angeles (UCLA), respectively, he spent eleven years honing professional skills at the Los Angeles office of Skidmore, Owings & Merrill prior to founding his own practice.

Frink's commercial work includes renovation of the Geffen Theater in the Westwood section of Los Angeles, the interior design for Warner Bros. Digital Studio in Burbank, and interiors for Warner Bros. Online Studio. However, it is a large-scale residential project in Montecito that best represents his own prescribed design challenges. Built for clients who had lived previously in Philip Johnson's Wiley House in New Canaan, Connecticut, both the large villa and its illustrated pool house are designed to fit into a lush, sloping landscape with minimal disturbance to site. Reached by a footbridge that crosses a dry creek and links the smaller structure to an infinity pool and terrace of the main house, the pool house is a finely wrought gem. It incorporates a full range of services within an 800-square-foot (72-square-meter), two-floor volume that sacrifices nothing in terms of crisp, modern style.

(left) A 50-foot-long (15-meter-long) bridge, supported by concrete piers on each end, wends through a wooded site to connect the pool house with the main residence. A wood deck extends from the main floor to expand the living area.

(opposite) Within the compact space, Frink made the grand gesture of a spiral stairway, constructed with a plaster railing wall and maple plank treads. Casual seating backs the more formal Barcelona table. Photos: Fotoworks—Benny Chan

(above) Living, dining, kitchen, and sleeping areas make the pool house a true home. A jukebox from the 1950s is incorporated into custom maple millwork in the living area.

(opposite) Double-height, gridded fenestration allows daylight infiltration while providing surface interest. The framing system and flooring throughout the house are of maple. Photos: Fotoworks—Benny Chan

j. frank
fitzgibbons

A modernist architect trained through apprenticeships with masters of the profession, Frank Fitzgibbons brings unexpected qualities of humanizing joy and warmth to the idiom. His residences are composed of strong, sculptural volumes that, through orientation and fenestration, take advantage of southern California's glorious sunlight. Inside, his spaces move fluidly, one into the other without any of the rigidity associated with die-hard modernism. But it is his unabashed use of saturated color that distinguishes Fitzgibbons from his colleagues with similar predilections. No beige-on-beige or "twenty shades of white" interiors for him.

Fitzgibbons originally intended to pursue graduate studies in urban design on fellowship at Pratt Institute. When the program was altered, he turned down the scholarship and devised his own graduate program where he would work with the some of the best modern architects of the time— Marcel Breuer, Romaldo Giurgola, and Richard Meier. He then spent eight years in Europe where he not only worked in Bern, Switzerland, and in Rome, but also studied painting, drawing, and sculpture. Fitzgibbons is an accomplished and exhibited artist as well as architect.

For the Rosenthal project, a 3,900-square-foot (351-square-meter) new house in Santa Monica, he cites color as the most important aesthetic element despite its complex composition of overlapping and intersecting planes. Interiors are sparked with grape railings, a chartreuse circular stair tower, a peach archway, and lemon end wall in the master bedroom. "Color," he says, "is applied atmospherically, diagrammatically, and emotionally."

(left) View from the dining room through a peach-colored archway to the living room, whose curvilinear furniture offsets the house's linear geometry.

(opposite) Dividing the living and dining rooms, the entry foyer is dominated by a chartreuse stair tower capped by a triangular skylight.
Photos: Toshi Yoshimi

(above) A yellow niche, backing a custom console, is focal point of the master bedroom.

(opposite) Exterior view from the children's balcony to the magenta stair tower. Photos: Toshi Yoshimi

(above) Exterior view of addition to renovated ranch house in Los Angeles' Laurel Canyon.

(opposite) The master bath addition to a Laurel Canyon residence is dominated by a south-facing window wall. The tub below the window is set into a honed limestone platform, which not only provides a bench for the adjacent double shower, but also extends outside. Photos: Joshua White

Susan Frank and David Frisch, 1988 graduates of the University of Arizona's School of Architecture, bring youth, exuberance, and diversified talents to their work. Now married and professional partners for the past seven years, the couple began their practice designing furniture. Design led to manufacturing; manufacturing aroused a special interest in metal fabrication. Through their own metalwork shop, Frank and Frisch completed commissions for other designers and architects as well as their own jobs. Their prestigious client list includes key players in the media and entertainment business: Paramount Pictures, Sony Studios, Mad River Post Production, Condé/Nast, and Chiat/Day. "Having a foot in the construction side of the business," they say, "gives us an insight into building."

As a firm, Frank + Frisch has grown to include its own architecture and design clients. For the Santa Monica beach condominium illustrated, the principals imparted architectural detailing and a sense of substance to a nondescript interior. Using Venetian plaster wall niches in unexpected locations, cherry doors and framing, patinated metals, and a newly created aperture between living room and bedroom for a view to the sea, they created perceptions of greater scale and more eye appeal. A second large-scale endeavor is the renovation of a 1950s ranch-style house in Laurel Canyon near Los Angeles. The commission began with just a master bath addition, but eventually grew to encompass a complete redo of the entire house. Large residential and commercial projects, however, have not precluded the carefully wrought interior in which Frank and Frisch perform their expertise in furniture design and metal fabrication. These experiments, such as the Kolsrud library for a film producer and his wife, allow the designers to hone their skills on diverse levels.

Susan Frank and David Frisch are the authors of the book, Metal: Design and Fabrication. Additionally, they divide their time between teaching at Los Angeles' Art Center College of Design and developing lighting products with a local manufacturer. "We also spend time," they say, "on some purely speculative projects as a vehicle for recharging our batteries and looking in new directions."

(opposite) Tinted stucco walls, custom maple and cherry cabinetry, and patinated metals such as the copper and blackened-steel fireplace wall elevate a once nondescript Santa Monica condominium to a little jewel box.

(above, left) Illuminated wall niches in the Santa Monica residence accommodate the client's objects collected during world travels. Cherry-framed French doors lead to the master bedroom.

(above, right) Since the only ocean view was from the bedroom, Frank and Frisch punctured the dividing wall to the living room so that both rooms would have access to the view. Photos: Joshua White

A library for a Los Angeles film producer and his wife has a custom cherry desk and Frank Gehry's iconic chair produced by Knoll. Detail illustrates the custom stainless-steel ladder, fabricated by the architects. Photos: Joshua White

giannetti architects

An architect whose residential buildings tend to evoke historical qualities of European counterparts, Stephen Giannetti draws on his heritage as a major influence. His grandfather, a master of ornamental plasterwork, emigrated from Bagni di Lucca in Tuscany to establish a studio in Maryland. He and hls two sons were commissioned for major restoration projects including the White House, the Supreme Court, and Jefferson's Monticello. Giannetti, since childhood, was raised with an appreciation of classical architecture.

After studying architecture at the University of Maryland, he began a professional career on the East Coast, which led to a friend's request for help on a shopping plaza in Beverly Hills. The Village on Canon, an Italian-inspired enclave built according to Giannetti's drawings, prompted his move to Los Angeles. On the West Coast, Giannetti established his practice in 1990, and has created more than seventy commercial and residential works to date. "I prefer to learn from history and as with a Porsche, refine and draw upon rich heritage," he comments. "Intelligence and emotion combine to make good architecture great."

His own residence in West Los Angeles illustrates not only his attraction to history, but also the villa-like qualities typical of his houses. Remodeling and expanding the original bungalow from 1,200 square feet to 2,500 square feet (108 square meters to 225 square meters), Giannetti transformed cramped, boxy rooms into an airy interior with ample room for a family of four. While the open, interflowing rooms of the remodeled living areas and the private spaces of a second-floor addition make the house functional, the finishes and decorative treatments render it charming. A welcome change from sleek, monochromatic interiors, this project is densely textured with saturated colors, decorative stenciling, ironwork, a plethora of patterns, quirky antiques, heirloom puti, and wife Brooke's numerous collections.

(left) A second-floor addition with board-and-batten construction is seamlessly integrated into the original bungalow. The stone patio and landscaping are also new.

(opposite) View through archway to the contiguous dining and family rooms. Features include newly installed beams, radiant heated concrete flooring plus custom designed chairs and lamps. Photos: Alex Vertikoff

(left) In the living room rich with pattern and texture, the owners' collections are displayed on original bungalow shelving. The finish was achieved by using mud, spiked with diluted paint, over drywall as a cost-efficient alternative to tinted plaster.

(below) The nook in the master bath was created expressly for Brooke's antique vanity that is topped by a collection of vintage handbags. Pedestal sinks, framed-mirror cabinets, and tumbled marble impart an old-world feeling Photos: Alex Vertikoff

hedge
design collective

Intent on developing an alternative to the conventional evolution of architecture student to professional practitioner, eighteen graduates of Los Angeles' SCI-Arc (Southern California Institute of Architecture) formed a collaborative venture. Hedge was founded in the spring of 1995. Mutual support, trust in the exchange of ideas, creativity, and invention are the concepts on which the studio operates. The paradigm answers the question team members asked on graduation: "How can we enter the workforce without throwing away what is potentially our most valuable asset?" By abstracting the educational environment into practice and surrounding themselves with a jury of peers, Hedge designers consistently challenge themselves, their level of thought, and quality of work.

With their diversity of backgrounds and interests, the designers and architects have engaged in a wide scope of work spanning design disciplines. Architecture projects, product and industrial design, exhibition and set design, landscape and urban projects, plus graphics all compose a body of completed work. Partners collaborate in changing teams based on how skills mesh with the project at hand. Illustrations show a range of residential interiors—the addition to and remodeling of a Santa Monica tract house, the conversion of an unused attic into a loft space in a Venice residence, and the renovation of a cramped 1,400-square-foot (126-square-meter) bungalow into an airy space.

(left) With its deep red end wall enlivened by the setting sun, the dining room addition is contiguous with the kitchen and living room. A skylight and heavy timber beams impart architectural detailing; triple sliding doors lead to a courtyard.

(opposite) Jackson Butler's commission for the Barry/Minardos project in Santa Monica entailed building a 400-square-foot (36-square-meter) master bedroom/bath addition and remodeling the rest of the 1,250-square-foot (112.5-square-meter) residence. A pivoting door connects the bedroom to the cast-in-place concrete koi pond. The balcony has views to the ocean. Photos: Marvin Rand

(above) Dave Maynard and Jackson Butler used skylights and express-ive forms in remodeling a Hollywood bungalow. Photo: Jackson Butler

(opposite) Inspired by Donald Judd, John Hirsch built a striking steel stairway for a Venice beach house to integrate the remodeled living room and previously unused attic. Photo: Mike Ferguson

william
hefner

An architect by training, William Hefner is as concerned with interior spaces as he is with physical structure. His design methodology, he says, is based on "working from the inside to the outside of the building." His projects, therefore, are characterized by rational plans with spaces connected both to each other and to the outdoors. A modernist, Hefner favors the use of materials to define spaces. "Although varied in style and project type," he says, "my work is marked by a quest for timeless elegance, an appreciation of the craft of building, and the use of natural materials."

Hefner founded his office in 1989 following undergraduate training in art history (including a year of study in Greece), a graduate degree in architecture from UCLA, and eight years with Skidmore, Owings & Merrill. In addition to private residences, which account for most of his practice, he has completed office and restaurant interiors and retail buildings. Geographically, his work is national and international in scope, with projects located in New York; Washington, D.C.; Sun Valley, Idaho; and Seoul, South Korea.

(left) The entry, expertly crafted in cherry wood paneling with maple reveals and maple flooring, complements the client's Asian pieces.

(opposite) Designing a new 2,000-square-foot (180-square-meter) apartment within the shell of a Beverly Hills high-rise, Hefner created a loft-like flow among rooms and integrated the balcony into the living area. The shoji screen treatment conceals a building column. Photos: Grey Crawford

(left) The master bedroom of a newly built residence in Claircrest, California, shows a sensitive articulation of sleeping and sitting quarters.

(below) Room-like in proportions and detailing, the master dressing area contains a large expanse of mirror and a built-in maple storage unit that extends into closets at left and right. Photos: Mark Lohman

(above) A bar made of Douglas fir veneers is the geographical center of the Lehrer house and gathering point for entertainment. Upstairs, a curved plaster wall is cut away to provide a view into the living space from the master suite.

(opposite) The Lehrer living room shows the stair tower and sunken conversation pit with built-in furniture, foreground. Two sliding doors open to the outside where polished black concrete helps blur the distinction between interior and exterior. Photos: Tom Bonner

"To craft the contemporary home is to understand and overcome the obstacles of interpersonal communications." This is the stated mantra of David Hertz, whose interdisciplinary and poetic approach to architecture and design is evident in his built projects, furniture designs, public sculpture, and product development.

Hertz views his work in architecture as a problem-solving exercise. Each solution, he says, "evolves organically from the clues and specifics of the site and the client." Yet a concern for specific issues, which are particularly relevant to southern California, pervades his work. The interplay of artificial and natural light is crucial. So are the honest expression of materials and structure, and the incorporation of natural ventilation. Attuned to his environment, Hertz advocates energy and resource efficiency, ecologically correct products, and the integration of exterior and interior spaces. His homes consistently express a strong sense of structure. Yet within this dramatic framework are fluid, overlapping spaces never far from an outdoor connection.

He was influenced by the masters: Frank Lloyd Wright, John Lautner, the intensely Californian work of both Schindler and Neutra, and the case study houses. Frank Gehry, for whom Hertz worked, is also cited as influential, as are other contemporary artists and architects.

The McKinley residence, built on a tight site in Venice for himself, his wife, and three young children, is designed with solar-powered hot water, radiant heating, natural ventilation, and nontoxic finishes. Much of the interior makes a consistent statement with poured-in-place concrete walls, furniture, and floors; pigmented stucco; exposed fir framing; and Syndecrete, the lightweight, precast concrete he created. "In the spirit of Schindler and Neutra," he says, "the building takes advantage of the coastal climate by creating outdoor spaces, including a sleeping porch, outdoor fireplace, and multiple roof decks used for recreation."

Hertz used similar systems and materials for the 7,500-square-foot (675-square-meter) Lehrer residence in Bel Air. A dramatic and open living expanse has a sunken fireplace pit and is minimally furnished with built-ins. There is no clutter; nor are there obstructions to the views.

(above) The view from the dining to living room of the McKinley house
shows concrete flooring and concrete bench/wall. "High windows," says
Hertz, "allow for a continued ceiling plane to expand the sense of space."

(opposite) Translucent light columns in the Lehrer residence separate the
breakfast room and kitchen. Photos: Tom Bonner

Gary Hutton's academic background is in fine arts and environmental design; his current affinities lean toward conceptual art and handcraftsmanship. Together, these disciplines lend a unique perspective to his work. His interiors, he says, "tend to have a clean, sculptural quality with a quiet luxury and inventive use of materials. Because my work is artful and has an intellectual quality, my inspiration comes mostly from artists and architects." In fact, much of his most successful work results from collaboration with local architects.

With degrees from the University of California at Davis and the California College of Arts and Crafts, Hutton is a modernist at heart. Yet he relishes the challenge of designing traditional residences and, coincidentally, has seen his own live/work space become more traditional over time. "Both fine antiques and well-designed, contemporary furniture have their best qualities revealed by being placed in relationship to each other in a room. Juxtaposing old and new reveals the magic of each object." The illustrated residence, a 1961 Gardner Daily structure built for the late Whitney Warren and originally decorated by Billy Baldwin makes his point perfectly. The grand living room, 21 feet by 36 feet (6.3 meters by 10.8 meters) with a 17-foot-high (5.1-meter-high) ceiling, is furnished with antiques dating to the eighteenth and nineteenth centuries. The adjacent sunroom, however, is filled with Saarinen's Tulip table and chairs and casual, white upholstered seating. All look appropriate, and all complement each other.

Hutton's great joy of custom designing furnishings for each design project has evolved into a second career. He has a collection of upholstered pieces and case goods in national distribution to the trade. A practicing professional since 1980, he has also designed restaurants, hotels, offices, and retail installations.

(left) The bedroom is a study of contemporary forms and neutral colors.

(opposite) The library of the Telegraph Hill residence is furnished with custom chairs and Ciao side table. A wall of shelving housing the client's collection of pre-Columbian pottery separates the library and sunroom. Photos: John Sutton

(above) A gilded doorway marks the entry to a Telegraph Hill residence built for the late Whitney Warren. Eighteenth-century Russian dining chairs surround a nineteenth-century Swedish table. The Italian fireplace mantel dates to the eighteenth century as does the Russian chandelier.

(right) Hutton's ease with traditional and modern elements is seen in the adjoining salon and sunroom. The contemporary seating and Saarinen pieces are ideal complements to the formal antiques and large-scale, oval-back chairs created by the designer. The Cambodian Buddha dates to the sixth century. Photos: John Sutton

Led by architects Barbara Callas and Steven Shortridge, Israel Callas Shortridge continues the firm founded by the seminal California architect Franklin D. Israel. The firm has left its mark on the Los Angeles landscape with film studios—most notably Propaganda—and such institutions as the UCLA Revlon Breast Care Center, the UC Riverside Fine Arts Seismic Building, and the UCLA Psychiatry Research Facility.

In the residential arena, which includes projects in Florida, Tokyo, and London as well as southern California, the firm holds an impressive roster of new structures and remodeling projects. The work, according to Shortridge, "is based on a balance of dialectics—shelter and expanse, light and shadow, mass and plane." Taking cues from the site, ICSA's projects tend to have solid ground forms with freer roof forms unfolding across the landscape. "Beneath these broad cantilevers," says Shortridge, "spaces flow into one another and through glass planes to connect the interior with the exterior's views, space, and light."

Although vastly different in scale and scope, the pair of pictured residences shows the firm's concentration on form, plane, and material to define interior space that, in turn, is never disconnected from its exterior environment. The Dan house is a new construction, replacing the original destroyed in the Malibu fire of 1993. In form, it is a bar building capped by an impressive hipped metal roof, with ceiling dominance repeated in the interior scheme. Shortridge's own residence, in contrast, is the renovation of an existing 750-square-foot (67.5-square-meter) bungalow in Venice. Reorganizing the procession, Shortridge created a situation emphasizing the garden terrace and indoor/outdoor continuity.

(left) The master bedroom of the Dan residence has a strong beam structure and glass walls opening to the pool and gardens. The fireplace and television cabinet, a singular construction, anchor a corner of the room.

(opposite) The living area of the Dan house in Malibu, California, flows into the den and kitchen areas beyond. Soffits and skylights define function zones. Photos: Erhard Pfeiffer

(above) The main living area of the Shortridge residence in Venice, California, shows the combination of old and new. The existing break-front was relocated to create a boundary with the kitchen; a new tongue-and-groove Douglas fir ceiling defines the conversation area.

(opposite) The dressing hall of the Shortridge house is defined by multi-function cabinetry of medium density fiberboard and Douglas fir veneer. Beyond, the bedroom can be closed off by an existing pocket door.
Photos: Stephen Oxenbury

Kanner Architects is a third-generation practice. Founded by Herman Kanner in 1946, then headed by son Chuck until his death in 1998, the firm now operates under the direction of Stephen Kanner, strongly influenced by his father/mentor/friend. Both Kanners, père and fils, were Los Angeles born and educated, and fell under the city's spell. Its iconic architecture, signage, graphics, car culture, and sheer exuberance affected the Kanners' two- and three-dimensional work, as both were prodigious painters as well as architects.

A multidiscipline organization creating a range of commercial and residential projects plus urban planning schemes, Kanner Architects is best known for its embrace of Googie style with its spirit of playfulness that distinguishes both architectural form and interiors. The aesthetic is particularly obvious in the firm's commercial structures such as multifamily housing units and the landmark In 'N Out Burger shop near the UCLA campus in Westwood. "Above all, the work," says Stephen Kanner, "conveys a sense of optimism."

His residences, many of them concentrated in Malibu, tend to follow a more serious, contemporary vein as a rational response to site conditions, proximity to the sea and local regulations. The Morton residence, created for a world-renowned oncologist and his family, is a 5,000-square-foot (450-square-meter) concrete structure whose south beach façade is glazed in a 13-foot (3.9-meter) grid. Inside, the space is organized on three stories; the main living area is an open expanse articulated only through slight level changes. Consistent finish materials, consideration of internal plus external views, and classical furnishings, albeit with a twist, characterize the interior solution.

The 5,000-square-foot (450-square-meter) Malibu residence has its entire beach façade glazed with doors opening onto wooden decks. The transparent elevation glows at night. Photos: Erhard Pfeiffer

Contiguous living and dining areas, with cherry flooring and mahogany framing, are furnished with Mies classics. Barcelona chairs are enlivened with red leather to complement the painterly custom rug.
Photos: Erhard Pfeiffer

(above) Mahogany cabinetry and black granite counters define a compact kitchen, a few steps down from the main living space.

(opposite) Cararra marble, suspended shelving, and a frameless glass shower enclosure contribute to a sense of openness in the master bath. Photos: Erhard Pfeiffer

The illustrated rooms show the variety of Craig Leavitt's and Stephen Weaver's work. These are designers who embrace bold strokes and are as equally at home with cutting-edge statements as with ornate and traditional décor. In each case, their project aims to strike a balance between envelope and furnishings. Backgrounds and architectural elements are rarely recessive. Instead, they are distinctly rendered as textural frameworks for the one-off objects Leavitt and Weaver design to fill their interiors. Even the sparsest of rooms is intricately textured.

Craig Leavitt and Stephen Weaver came together in 1976 with diverse backgrounds and individual strengths, facts that made them successful partners. Weaver's background is in painting and psychology; Leavitt's is interior design having worked with Tony Hail in San Francisco and Parrish-Hadley in New York. Weaver sees the broad picture and "cleans out rooms for comfort," he says. Leavitt delights in details, the intricacies of decorating and shopping, which he calls collecting. Together the two edit each other; the result, they say, "is one great designer."

Before embarking on the Getty project, one of their most ambitious endeavors, Leavitt/Weaver already had an impressive project roster—a marketed furniture collection, residences; a private Boeing 727; and a Squaw Valley inn, cafés, and wine shops for the PlumpJack Management Group. In remodeling a 5,500-square-foot (495-square-meter) penthouse with panoramic views for Getty family scion Billy, the partners completed a comprehensive work of architecture. The San Francisco space was razed to its structural elements and articulated through a system of translucent sliding panels and suspended ceiling "wafers," all arrayed on a circular plan. There are no doors or conventional walls; nor is there hanging art to compete with the views. The expansiveness, concrete flooring, and exposed beams allude to a loft vocabulary whose intentionally rough state is counter-balanced by luxurious custom furniture with roots in the moderne period.

(left) One of the seating areas in the Getty apartment is defined by a curved sofa upholstered in a 1920 Parisian Art Deco carpet runner. Leather squares are pieced together to form a rug. Photo: Ira Nowinski/Leavitt Weaver

(opposite) To complement a client's existing collection of seventeenth- and eighteenth-century furniture, the partners created a room of Coromandel screens, gilt moldings, and silk wall upholstery, all of it newly made. Photo: David Duncan Livingston

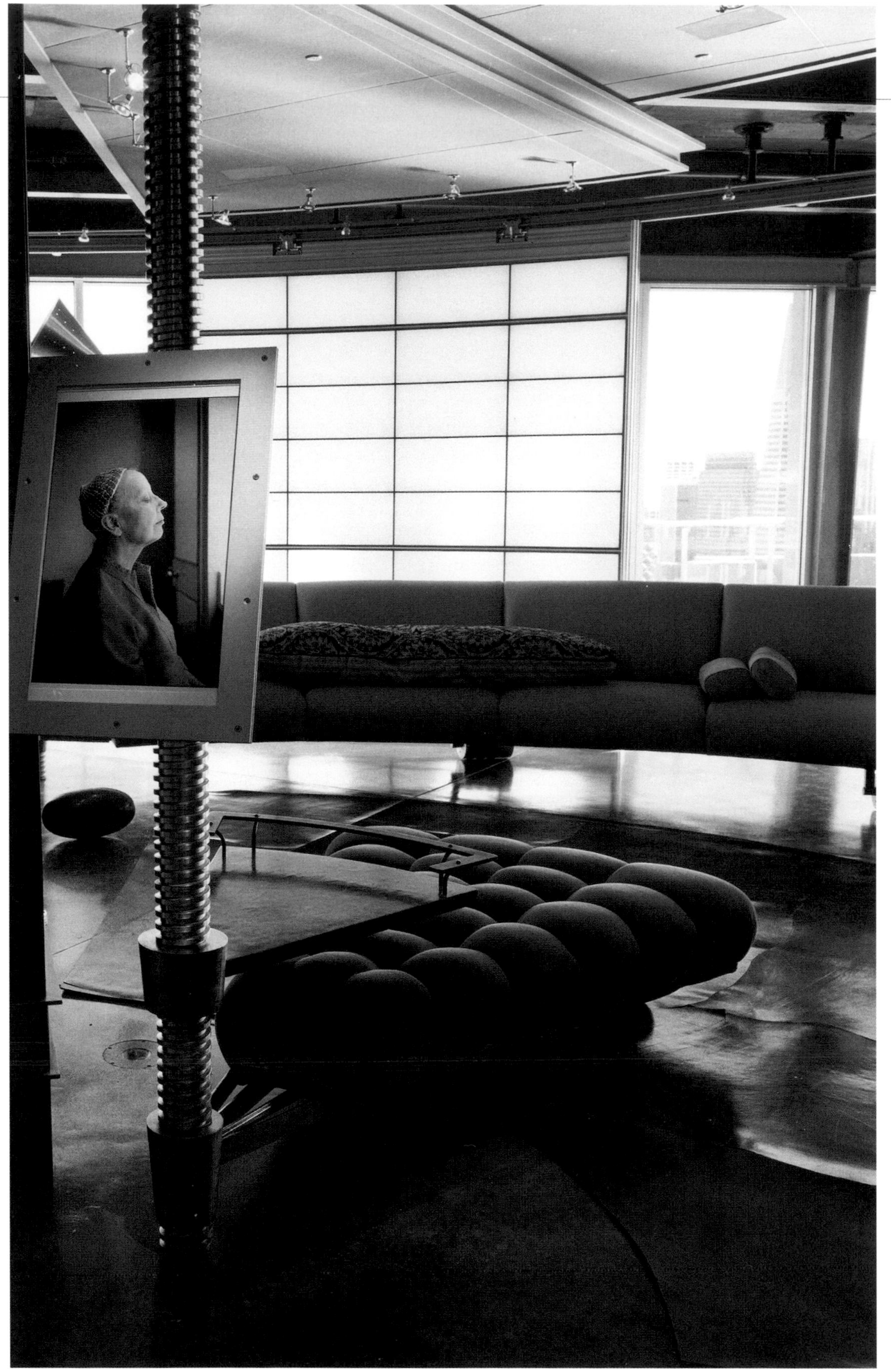

(left) **The seating area at one fireplace consists of a pivoting sofa
and overscaled ottoman, both designed by Leavitt/Weaver.**

(below) **The master-bath view shows a tub encased in a concrete shell,
a cast rock-face wall, and the partition system that confers privacy.**
Photos: Ira Nowinski/ Levitt Weaver

No book on West Coast design and architecture would be complete without Morphosis and its founder Thom Mayne. He and his firm were instrumental in bringing contemporary California architecture to worldwide attention. Established in 1972 on the premise that design is a collective enterprise, Morphosis, to date, has received fifty awards for design excellence from professional journals and organizations.

Each Morphosis project—whether it be a school such as the Diamond Ranch High School, an office interior like Friedland Jacobson Advertising, an international conference/ trade center in China, or a house such as the Blades residence shown here—is a team effort. "Our ideals," says Mayne, "are built on the premise that design is not a matter of compromise between functional and aesthetic concerns, rather that the aesthetics are driven by human activity and utility made evident."

Design, for Morphosis, is a problem-solving experience. Each project has its own context and merit; each deserves a creative solution eschewing preconceptions and dogma. Consistently, concepts are developed through consideration: of the effect of scale and architectural elements on the surrounding area; of an organic equilibrium between new and existing architecture; of creating a new presence that seems to belong to the site. Working methods involve the extensive use of large-scale physical and computer models to identify potential prob-lems and explore alternative solutions throughout the process.

(left) View of the fireplace of the Blades residence, in Santa Barbara, California, which dominates the living area as a sculptural gesture.

(opposite) The 4,500-square-foot (405-square-meter) Blades residence addresses the clients' request for interconnected, open zones for living/kitchen/dining, studio/gallery, and bedroom. "A large exterior room has been created within which the house is situated," says Mayne.
Photos: Kım Zwarts

Additional views show the use of strong forms and materials to articulate interior space in lieu of traditional walls and furnishings. Constructed for $620,000, the house won a 1997 California Chapter AIA award. Photos: Kim Zwarts

brian alfred murphy

Twenty years ago, when Brian Murphy first began to practice, he was called "the bad boy of architecture." Some thought he was purely after shock value. Time, however, has validated Murphy's approach as his projects remain fresher than ever. Strong and idiosyncratic, his houses defy identification or a single architectural stamp. He may build in a constructivist manner with strong and often twisted concrete geometric forms, abundantly punctured with windows and skylights. Or, he is equally comfortable with a simpler vernacular. Murphy can take a classic bungalow or shed design and make it his own through scale, massing, or detail. His homes are consistently witty with a sparkling sense of humor. They display an industrial edge without slavish adherence to a minimalist aesthetic, and evince a built quality. His interior rooms are delightful compositions of objects—some of them formal, some of them found, some of them Murphy fabrications.

Murphy has a deeply ingrained knowledge of construction. His father was a contractor, and he tagged along to construction sites from early childhood. Later, he engrossed himself in the trade as a carpenter and builder. Practical experience led to formal training. He was an art major at UCLA, went to L.A. Trade Tech and the UCLA Graduate School of Architecture and Urban Planning. A hands-on professional, Murphy's comprehension of construction techniques assures that his projects are not only creative, but also feasible and cost effective.

(left, top) Murphy's concept of rooms extends to the exterior with its concrete terrace.

(left) Glass dining table appears to float thanks to its overhead metal support structure. Metal track allows the TV to slide the length of the room. Murphy's innovative industrial lighting is his only trademark.

(opposite) The open living room is enlivened by a series of diverse skylights and a gold-plated steel "diamond" that screens powder and coat rooms from the public space. Photos: Tim Street-Porter

The front door, when open, becomes a partial frame for the stairway.
The sleeping area is a witty take on formality. Photos: Tim Street-Porter

(opposite) A full-height panel of translucent glass suggests separation between dining and living zones in a Pacific Palisades residence. The glass-topped coffee table is supported by columns of inverted flower pots.

(below) Murphy transformed nondescript wood flooring into a focal point with marine blue aniline dye. The table is made from window grating retrieved from a junkyard, and one leg is a baseball bat. Ordinary Christmas lighting—wadded up—becomes a chandelier in Murphy's hands. Photos: Tim Street-Porter

Based in Seattle, but with projects completed nationwide, Olson Sundberg is profoundly affected by its Northwest location. "The suffused and rich quality of light here is powerful in its ability to reveal and conceal form. The landscape is both open and closed, creating densely layered vistas, and there is a way of life here that is closely attuned to this environment and its natural patterns. Our design approach responds to these natural elements."

The firm's projects—whether they are institutional buildings, museums, private residences, or interiors—thus share these philosophical traits. Forms are carefully articulated. Interior space typically has an ambiguous quality extending beyond physical boundaries. Interior forms are dissolved through combinations of visually floating ceiling planes, careful control of daylight, and obscured connections between solids and voids."

Olson Sundberg interiors present a dense study in materials, textures, and details. Glass is vital for its translucence that defies materiality and ties a room to its exterior surroundings. Metal is prevalent in many rooms. It, too, can become dematerialized as illustrated by the Blem condominium. The predominant use of steel—as an entry wall, much of the flooring, and cladding for freestanding storage modules, fireplace, kitchen, and bath—renders physical boundaries ambiguous thanks to its reflective surface. Metal also holds fascination for its acquired patina that changes with use over time.

Concerned with context, place, and physical and spiritual comfort, the architects extend their explorations to an interest in art. "Art has the ability to transcend everyday existence and material considerations and lead to what is important in our lives."

(left) Stainless steel clads the fireplace and much of the Seattle apartment's surfaces to perceptually break down the boundaries of the space. Photo: Eduardo Calderon

(opposite) A two-story space is used as both the main living area and a photography studio in the Margolis residence in Seattle. Full-height pivot doors within the gridded glass wall open interior space to the outdoors. Photo: Paul Warchol

(above) The kitchen island of the Blem residence, which has views of both the Space Needle and Mount Rainier, is a tapering plane of stainless steel, supported on the end by a suspended metal bar. This polished composition of Manhattan-like elegance is a counterpoint to the relaxed and organic interiors characteristic of Seattle.

(opposite) Freestanding storage modules, sheathed in perforated metal and supported by floor-to-ceiling steel brackets, separate public and private zones in the 2,600-square-foot (234-square-meter) Blem condominium. Photos: Eduardo Calderon

polly osborne and john erickson

Polly Osborne and John Erickson are independent practitioners and frequent collaborators as a result of similar backgrounds and shared ideas. Both are SCI-Arc graduates; both consider themselves "green" architects with a particular responsibility to the environment. "Our focus," they say, "is site-specific architecture with minimal impact on the environment and maximum health, beauty, and harmony to our client. We are hands-on architects, designing furniture and fixtures as well as space."

Their approach is particularly suited to residential renovation. These projects test their skills in analyzing existing spaces, restructuring them and meshing them with additions. For a 1926 Mediterranean house in the Los Feliz section of Los Angeles, they confronted a structure whose previous five additions had compromised its integrity. Before Osborne and Erickson could restore the house to its aesthetic roots and add the requested spaces for kitchen, dining room, master suite, and patio, they demolished these prior interventions. The exterior was refinished, appropriately, with stucco and tile. New interior finishes consist of cherry, oak, chingapin wood, and Malibu tile, which provide a complementary background to the owner's collection of Craftsman furnishings.

Similarly, Osborne and Erickson respected the origins of another 1920s residence, once the home of a speakeasy, in renovating it for family living. Retaining the original footprint, they reapportioned space to accommodate a new den— impeccably crafted in bird's-eye maple and cherry—and bath. They also installed new windows for light and garden views plus created backgrounds, finishes, and detailing, all in keeping with the house's original sense of substance.

(left) Osborne and Erickson built a new dining room with barrel vaulted ceiling and doors to the outside gardens for the Los Feliz residence. Built-in drawers solve a storage problem.

(opposite) The living room of the Los Feliz residence, a light-filled space with a newly vaulted ceiling, houses the owner's collection of Craftsman furnishings. Photos: Tim Street-Porter

(opposite) The interior den in the speakeasy renovation is fitted with cabinetry whose shallow width is belied by the richness of bird's-eye maple and cherry woods. Drawer pulls were hand-carved by the architects. Photo: Derek Rath

(below) The master suite is situated in the new section of the Los Feliz house. Utterly simple with pine flooring and cedar ceiling, the room's focal point is a Japanese screen suspended from the ceiling to front the plaster fireplace. Photo: Tim Street-Porter

antoine predock

Based in Albuquerque, Antoine Predock is known for architecture inspired by site and surrounding culture. While his buildings may make bold strokes in the landscape, they consistently respond to the idiosyncrasies of program.

Built on a suburban street in Manhattan Beach, California, where the plots are notoriously compact, the Rosenthal house is an oxymoron of complex simplicity. A bold composition of opaque and transparent geometric forms, the house is described by Predock as "a kind of excavated Rubik's Cube" for its client, a freelance toy designer. "It presents the possibility of many different interlocking interior/ exterior spatial relationships within a discrete geometric envelope." The three-story volume is organized with a kitchen/ living zone on the ground floor, an open studio on the middle level, and a lantern-like sleeping/study area on top. All are accessible by interior and exterior stairways. Each zone works individually or as part of the whole.

Predock has been practicing architecture since 1967. Internationally acclaimed with numerous AIA and other awards, he is a Rome Prize Fellow, a fellow of the American Institute of Architects, a professor and lecturer, a critic, and the subject of two monographs. His commercial works span the globe. A small sampling includes: the Nelson Fine Arts Center, Arizona; the Palm Bay complex, Morocco; the National Archives of Denmark; the Arizona Science Center in Phoenix; and the Spencer Theater for the Performing Arts in Ruidoso, New Mexico.

(left, above) Given the transparency of the Rosenthal house, interior and exterior stairways appear to intersect as kinetic sculpture.

(left) The house is oriented so that its perimeter walls, balconies, and stairways provide intersecting views that include the surrounding Manhattan Beach, California, neighborhood and the Pacific Ocean.

(opposite) The ground-level interior is a sparsely furnished living zone with Italian seating and Starck-designed chairs. Photos: Timothy Hursley

In the private top floor, "sliding-glass panels inside the exterior glass perimeter can render the entire southern elevation translucent or overlap to create different levels of opacity," Predock explains. The X-bracing in transparent glass walls addresses seismic codes. Photos: Timothy Hursley

"Our approach to design takes place on two basic levels," say Gwynne Pugh and Lawrence Scarpa, partners in the architecture/design/engineering firm founded in 1984. "The first is a set of fundamental philosophical attitudes about what to do; the second, a concern with appropriate design decisions and how to implement them." Whatever the projects, Pugh + Scarpa consider the same elements crucial to the problem-solving process. Structure, program, materials, and organization of form, space, and light factor into every decision. The firm emphasizes a team approach; a principal is involved in every project.

The partners bring to their projects an edgy, modern attitude stemming from their diverse international backgrounds. Pugh was educated at Leeds University in Britain and UCLA in Los Angeles. Scarpa, who holds previous experience in the offices of Gene Leedy and Paul Rudolph, lived in Italy after receiving a traveling research fellowship to study the work of Carlo Scarpa and teach in Vicenza.

Pugh and Scarpa attempt to break the mold. But the solution, however, outré, must work. For the Simenhoff project, a new 1,300-square-foot (117-square-meter) master bedroom suite and renovation of the public living spaces, Pugh + Scarpa brought a typical 1940s tract house into the realms of contemporary architecture by expressing and exaggerating typical elements of door, windows, columns, fireplace elevation, and ceiling. The stairway becomes a means of tying the interiors to the exterior view. The Jassim residence, a newly built weekend retreat surrounded by the Los Padres national forest, integrates traditional cabin imagery with a clean, modern interior and concern for views.

(left) A 1940s tract house is made contemporary by expressing its architectural elements with copper siding, cement plaster, exposed wood, and concrete.

(opposite) An equally strong sense of structure pervades interiors of the renovated Simenhoff residence. Modern icons of different eras— Le Corbusier's Gran Confort seating and Philippe Starck's Café Costes chairs—sit side by side. Photos: Marvin Rand

(above) A traditional cabin from the exterior, the Jassim weekend retreat has an open modern interior dominated by a pair of glass garage doors opening the living room to the site. Photos: Marvin Rand

(opposite) A stair landing ties the interior to the view in a renovated residence. Photos: Marvin Rand

Founded in 1985, Rios Associates resembles a European paradigm in its organization and approach to design. Under the direction of Mark Rios, Julie Smith, and Frank Clementi, the studio is an interdisciplinary firm operating in a team-oriented environment. Landscape architecture plus furniture design and graphics typically figure into a project's scope, augmenting interior design and architecture. This interdisciplinary approach to the design process, "allows us to offer a holistic vision for each project," Rios comments.

The goals of modernism form the basis of the firm's design philosophy. Yet, modernism as defined by Rios and his team is not the austere, elite aesthetic common to popular perception. As interpreted here, it is "a rich, eclectic, and hopeful spirit exemplified by California Case Study modernism." The Smith-Clementi residence, representing the renovation and expansion of a 600-square-foot (54-square-meter) bungalow dating to the 1920s, illustrates a melding of modernism's pragmatism with qualities of youthful exuberance. The residence is warm, inviting, and filled with the personalities of the couple and their young daughter. Similarly, the Taplin house shows the transformation of a '50s-style suburban ranch into "a more layered spatial experience" that extends to the grounds. By raising the roof, opening up the floor, dematerializing the southern barrier with a glass elevation, and continuing the limestone flooring outside, the firm's design team created an indoor/outdoor situation inherent in southern California living.

Mark Rios stresses the design process. "It begins in a cyclical, nonlinear pattern of listening to clients, of research, of program development, of communication and prioritizing design goals," he says. The work, therefore, is based on collaboration between team members and client. Solutions are based on a clearly perceived idea. Forms and structures, furniture and detailing are honest and integrated. Gestures are sometimes grand, sometimes humble, sometimes fun. They are never fancy, repetitive or part of a stock solution.

(above) Laminate-faced kitchen cabinetry in the Smith-Clementi residence alludes to the firm's expertise in graphics and its sense of fun.

(opposite) Julie Smith and Frank Clementi transformed a 600-square-foot (54-square-meter), uninsulated shack into a charming two-floor home, true to the bungalow vernacular of surrounding structures on a walk-street in Venice. Casement and clerestory windows provide light and amplify the volume. The wheeled sofa is a custom design. Photos. Tom Bonner

(opposite) The living/dining space of the renovated Taplin residence presents a serene study in color and materials. Limestone flooring and maple woodwork at the fireplace influenced color for the framework of the focal wall. "The client appreciated architect and designer furnishings, be they original 1950s to 1960s pieces or furniture designed now," says Rios. A vintage Heywood-Wakefield dining set works well with upholstered pieces in current production. Photo: Derek Rath

(below) The master bedroom in the Smith-Clementi residence is part of a second-floor addition. Solid walls come to a high mark of four and one half feet (1.35 meters). Windows provide panoramic views of the sky and seventy-year-old magnolia tree next door. Photo: Tom Bonner

(above) A new double-height entry in the Taplin residence in Los Angeles is detailed with sandblasted glass panes. The glass and steel lighting fixture, designed by Rios Associates, has stylistic roots in a Japanese lantern.

(opposite) In the interest of harmony, the bedroom of the Taplin house is a continuation of the color/materials palette. Photos: Derek Rath

Change, research, and practice. These are the words founding partner Michael Hricak uses to describe his firm's work. One of Los Angeles' most prolific architecture studios, Rockefeller/Hricak, designs and builds residences as contemporary solutions to the particulars imposed by site and program. The ideas are consistently clear and fresh; they are, however, never an arbitrary decision meant to make a stylistic statement.

"Our work continues to change, less by choice and more from a search for an approach to the making of buildings and finding delight in the possibilities of the program, materials, methods, and the design of the information necessary to bring about our intentions," says Hricak. Process is as important as product. "We are fascinated by how things are made, of what are they made, and the result when program comes in contact with our own ideas and experiences. In our practice we do just that, practice by doing over and over until we develop a sense of understanding of the built results of our ideas."

If the firm's projects share common traits, they can be seen in the pictured Silverman and Thue residences. The Silverman house is a grand 6,300-square-foot (567-square-meter) residence designed, Hricak says, "as a series of buildings that recalls the architectural legacy of the historic Rustic Canyon district" of Los Angeles. The Thue house is a compact 2,300-square-feet (207-square-meter) house in Manhattan Beach. Both, however, display a strong sense of structure, articulation, and level change to maximize views and connection to the outside. In both cases, the finely wrought interior architecture encompasses detailed cabinetry and the sensitive use of glass, stone, and plaster in the materials palette.

Added to a concern for process and product is that of longevity. "We are as interested," says Hricak, "with how our work ages and weathers, how it is used today and over time."

(above) A two-story gallery is the main circulation element in the Silverman project. It separates the public zones from the two private bedrooms, each with a bath. The master suite occupies the third of the house's three levels.

(opposite) Constructed on a tight 30- by 45-foot (9- by 13.5-meter) lot in Manhattan Beach, the Thue residence is crafted like a finely built ship that "takes full advantage of the natural light, views, and breezes unique to the coastal environment of southern California," Hricak says. The main loft space on the upper level is wrapped with windows allowing a 360-degree panorama. Photos: David Glomb

View of the double-height fireplace elevation and detail of cabinetry in the Silverman residence located in Rustic Canyon, which is bordered by the Pacific Ocean and Santa Monica mountains. All rooms in the house open directly to balconies, decks, or patios. Photos: David Glomb

Though Seccombe Design Associates may be best known for its commercial work, its tour-de-force is a residence. The complete restructuring of a Pacific Heights (San Francisco) house for a Silicon Valley magnate is a tough job to top—in terms of all design-related disciplines.

Built in 1961 on a site offering heart-stopping views of the San Francisco Bay stretching from the Golden Gate Bridge to Alcatraz, the house was large at 10,000 square-feet (900 square meters) with adequate volume on the first floor. However, it lacked the interior glamour to stand up to both the views and the client's status as a captain of computer technology and a world-class host. It also held no vestiges of the Japanese culture with which he is enamored. The designer's job, with architect T. Olle Lundberg, was to address all deficits through a program of restructuring, finishes, and furnishings.

A front courtyard, dominated by a gravity-defying boulder fountain, marks the entry to the house whose façade was newly clad with off-white crystalline glass panels from Japan. From here, visitors enter with a new, canted glass and steel elevation providing smaller dramatic views of a second interior courtyard. The living room, at 1,000 square-feet (90 square meters), with a 12-foot (3.66-meter) high ceiling, had an entire wall of glass. Rather than leave an unarticulated expanse of glass, the designer and architect detailed it with French doors, steel mullions, louvred windows, and a truncated steel column to frame segments of the panorama.

The space implied a dichotomy. Grand scale is not always conducive to comfortable living and entertaining. Addressing both, Seccombe devised a simple plan grounded in the Asian tenets of simplicity and harmony, balance and purpose. Envelope materials are consistently stone or wood with a recurrent grid motif. Cream and white rule the color palette. Contemporary furnishings, sparsely deployed but often decadent with white leather or cream silk upholstery, form a dazzling interpretation of minimalism.

(above) From a gridded interior courtyard, the house is almost totally transparent. A ribbon stairway is of ash and stainless steel. Photos: Toshi Yoshimi

(opposite) Gridded paneling of English sycamore is a warm counterpoint to the guest bedroom's cool whiteness. Furniture classics are by Mies, Le Corbusier, and Charles Eames. Photos: Toshi Yoshimi

(above) A fiber-optic lighting strip is buried in a structural column behind the Italian desk.

(right) The window wall is broken up to frame segments of the view. Barcelona tables and seating from Antonio Citterio's Sity collection constitute most of the furnishings. Photos: Toshi Yoshimi

Founded in 1951, Sienna Architecture embraces design's various disciplines. The firm provides architecture, interior design, urban planning, and environmental graphics for clients throughout the western United States. Its projects range in scope from small, retail concept shops to town centers and thirty-story residential towers.

The firm's greatest strength, however, may well be its ability to interpret vernacular architecture. The pictured McKenzie River house in Eugene, Oregon, is a 4,800-square-foot (432-square-meter) residence that addresses the clients' dreams of a Cascadian Lodge, an Oregon ranch, and elements of the Pacific Rim. Constructed of materials from the environment—cedar siding, basalt stone, and vertical-grain fir—the house is dramatic in its open spaces, yet cozy through the abundant use of wood and rustic quality. The main living expanse—which includes sitting and dining areas and large, open kitchen—is overlooked by a loft whose railings are detailed with stylized Japanese motifs. The west wing accommodates a master suite and library; the east wing houses utility, storage, and fly-tying rooms. On the lower level are children's bedrooms, a playroom, and wine cellar. Throughout, there is access to views of the property's natural meadow.

(left) A fir and green steel spiral stairway is the connecting spine to the structure's three levels.

(opposite) A north-facing bay window provides a dramatic framework for the spiral stairway. Photos: John Hughel

(left) Fir beams and a basalt stone fireplace enhance the rustic contextualism of the house. The sitting area has views of the meadow and McKenzie River.

(below) Although lodge-like in atmosphere, the kitchen is equipped with state-of-the-art appliances. Photos: John Hughel

Sixteen years ago Beth Slifer, an MBA graduate of the University of Chicago and an assistant in Washington D.C.'s Environmental Protection Agency during the Carter administration, moved to Vail. While eminently qualified in other fields, she had no design training. But that didn't stop her from sprucing up a hard-to-sell condominium on a $17,000 budget from a local realtor. Within a week, the condo was sold, and Slifer found a second career. Combining her business acumen with information initially obtained from her designer mother, she began as a sole practitioner and stayed close to home in the Vail Valley.

Now Slifer Designs is a firm of more than sixty, whose staff of designers and architects offers new building as well as remodeling and decorating projects in both commercial and residential arenas. Slifer is currently ranked as number fourteen in the top 100 woman-owned companies in Colorado. Within the firm, Slifer attributes growth and success to teamwork. "As soon as I recognized the growth potential," she says, "it was obvious that we weren't going to be the typical interior design firm where there's one lead creative person or personality."

Slifer, in addition to accepting her own commissions, operates designer showrooms in Edwards and Aspen. The firm's location and financial prosperity make it a natural for resort commissions; the Beaver Creek Club and Roaring Fork Club and Cabins count among completed works. Location also figures prominently in Slifer's aesthetic. Oversized furniture, solid woods not veneers, natural fabrics, Oriental rugs, and offbeat accessories are components of a western look appealing to urban cowboys and sophisticates as well.

(left) An entry vignette in a Beaver Creek residence alludes to the area's western traditions with a bronze sculpture modeled after a Remington, its overscaled carved mirror and console and its iron lamps with antique parchment shades.

(opposite) Located lift-side at Vail, this condo's living room could be mistaken for a big-city counterpart with its antique buffet, chaise, and sofa covered with antique velvet, stainless-steel reading lamp, and series of framed botanical prints. Photos: David Marlowe

A grand living room with coffered ceiling and massive stone fireplace is designed for after-ski comfort in a slope-side estate in Beaver Creek. Abundant seating, all generous in scale, is anchored by a Tibetan rug.
Photo: David Marlowe

A native of New York and a graduate of that city's Parsons School of Design, Alisa Smith is a West Coast transplant. She began professional life as a color consultant on architecture and historic preservation projects, and her career has evolved into full-scale interior design. Smith practices both residential and commercial design; given her background, she is particularly sensitive to renovation projects. One of her most accomplished works is an award-winning project with historical and sentimental ties to old Hollywood. A vintage carpentry building, circa 1919, on Charlie Chaplin's old studio lot was given new life as the creative services department for A&M Records thanks to Smith's sensitive intervention. She received a 1998 citation from the Los Angeles Conservancy for her efforts.

In the residential arena, Smith's work spans Los Angeles, Pasadena, San Francisco, Seattle, and New York. "Color and lighting," she says, "are the foundation for all work. Simple solutions and functionalism are always primary concerns. I like furniture to look undesigned." Actor Ben Stiller's residence in a Hollywood landmark building shows her penchant for unadorned spaces that let architectural details and the few selected furnishings—usually antique or custom pieces—stand out. As for her unabashed love for color and exotic themes, nothing shows it better than the Moroccan-inspired dining room she shares with her writer husband and two young children.

(left, above) With views of Hollywood, the terrace functions as an additional room in Stiller's 3,000-square-foot (270-square-meter) penthouse. Plantings were installed to provide privacy on one side and maximize the view on the other.

(left) The ceiling of the guest bedroom in Ben Stiller's Hollywood duplex is painted sky blue. A turn-of-the-century cast-iron daybed displays its natural finish.

(opposite) Stiller's duplex was originally occupied by George Raft. The living room is treated as a gallery for Stiller's photography collection. The dining room combines refined and industrial elegance. Photos: William Mackenzie-Smith

The dining room of Smith's 2,000-square-foot (180-square-meter) house, built in 1947, is a vivid Moroccan-themed space conducive to entertaining. Photo: William Mackenzie-Smith

john
staff

A native of Los Angeles, John Staff has built houses spanning the city's varied and widespread regions—from
Manhattan Beach with its restrictive lot sizes, to Malibu with
its issues posed by rough seas and salt air, to Santa Monica
with an ideal climate but tough zoning laws. Throughout, he
has created solutions responsive to site and an evolved
design consciousness. A Staff house may resemble a classic
Mediterranean, for example, but its proportions are tweaked
and its interior volumes typically stretch the limits of gen-
erosity. An appreciation for daylight marks all his projects.
Houses are detailed with skylights, clerestories, and
fenestration focusing on some of southern California's
incomparable views. Staff's interiors are consistently
detailed with fine cabinetry and built-in pieces regardless of
budget. In this sense, furniture is treated as part of the
architecture. Staff's background and his wife's own
contracting business explain this added dimension of his
architecture. He earned an undergraduate degree in art
with a furniture design emphasis from San Diego State
University and completed a master's degree in architecture
from SCI-Arc.

(left) Despite a limited furnishings budget for the Malibu beach house,
Staff created maple cabinetry and a marble fireplace in the master
bedroom.

(opposite) A home office with adjacent balcony faces the Pacific Ocean
in a newly constructed Malibu beach house. Strong framing and custom-
built furniture distinguish the room. Photos: J. Scott Smith

(above) Staff's house in Santa Monica is a sprawling 4,700-square-foot (423-square-meter) building with Mediterranean roots. The open kitchen, designed for entertaining as well as cooking, features a built-in bar to complement the work island.

(opposite) Staff introduced a series of eye-level windows to humanize the grand scale of the vaulted dining room in the house he shares with his wife and three young children. The antique table and chairs are a charming counterpoint to the contemporary architecture. Photos: J. Scott Smith

lenny steinberg

Although a native Californian, Lenny Steinberg embraces a particularly European approach towards design. Knowing that Italian architects are among her closest friends, one understands why. For her, design, whatever the medium, is related. "There is an unnecessary delineation in understanding and appreciating various art forms," she says. "Separation in the arts is an unfortunate blockage to both the creator and the observer. While the product may be different, theoretically the process and principles of composition are the same from one form to the next."

Steinberg works in many media, just as she draws references from a broad arts spectrum. Music and modern dance studies, had an impact on her own spatial awareness and all-over creative senses. She designs furniture, graphics, jewelry, costumes, and residential and commercial interiors. She has worked with Frank Gehry on a shopping center and a residence in Cheviot Hills, Los Angeles. Steinberg's own interiors have an architectural focus, where strong planes and forms take precedence over decorative embellishment. Furnishings are pared to essentials with built-in pieces favored. The Bain house, in the Hollywood Hills, shows not only Steinberg's aesthetic, but also the keen eye that enabled her to transform a sadly remodeled mess into a glamorous loft-like space revealing the clean post-and-beam construction of the original.

(left) For the library, a few steps below grade, Steinberg created a wall of cabinetry for books and TV. Custom tables are aluminum, detailed with antique blue bubble glass.

(opposite) Custom furnishings face a new fireplace wall. Seating frames are glass-blasted stainless steel. Photos: Tim Street-Porter

(above) The second-floor corridor has a custom ledge for art display.

(right) The master bedroom's new fireplace elevation incorporates a seating banquette. Metal tables were designed by Steinberg. Photos: Tim Street-Porter

A collaborator, an interpreter, and, an interior designer. With these as her priorities, Madeline Stuart certainly has no self-identifying stamp to her work. The only consistency is inconsistency. "I try not to repeat myself and to appreciate the fact that my clients want to feel as though I've spent time understanding who they are and what they want. If on a tour of my projects they saw the same lamp, fabric, dining chair, or end table, would they believe I had their best interest at heart or that I was just issuing them a uniform that fits all?"

Her projects span a broad stylistic range. She did an eccentric take on a Victorian theme for English stage actors with a venerable residence in Los Angeles's Hancock Park. For longtime client Lisa Henson's illustrated Mediterranean house in Beverly Hills, she brought in elements of Oriental and Moroccan luxury. Camp Lone Pine is an out-of-the-way ranch at the base of Mount Whitney in Owens Valley, California. "This is a place for reading and fires, hiking and cooking," she says. Her goal: to make it appear as if a decorator had never set foot in the place. Her own house, similarly undecorated, "is merely a collection of stuff that I buy with no other thought than I want it, need it, have to have it. I'm not certain I would ever combine these elements this way in a client's house."

Stuart's definition of a designer mixes professional and personal qualities. "I think the mark of a great designer," she says, "is the ability to combine a knowledge of materials (whether it be silk velvet or linoleum), a sense of humor (too much perfection and it lacks joy), and an appreciation of comfort and suitability with an understanding of scale and proportion. Add to that the ability to respond to and respect the architecture or space."

(left) Renovation discovered a portion of the original fireplace, embellished by Stuart with seventeenth-century Moroccan tiles. The addition of 10-foot-high (3-meter-high) French doors enhanced the opening to the gardens "in a true reflection of a California lifestyle."

(opposite) Lisa Henson's Mediterranean house was purchased in derelict condition and restored to an interpretation of its original 1930s sensibility. Fabrics are lush, custom upholstered pieces are generously proportioned; the rug is an antique Sultanabad. All, however, are supporting players to the dominant eighteenth-century gilt Japanese screen. Photos: Dominique Vorillon

"The resolve was to make Camp Lone Pine a real place—not just some concoction designed and conceived in accord with an aesthetic notion of what a ranch house should be," Stuart says. "However, if you look closely, you might find a headboard that was milled at the Disney Studio molding department or a Hodsoll McKenzie fabric from England." Photos: Dominique Vorillon

Rysia Suchecka is passionate about design and its ability to influence lives. As director of interiors for the Seattle-based architecture/design firm NBBJ, she has been responsible for hospitals, hotels, restaurants, offices, schools, and spas on an international basis. Whether the project is meant to heal, to educate, to make one look or feel good, or to work well, each is grounded in identical beliefs. "Design is real, not theory," she says, "not about taste or style or trend, but about permanent values."

Suchecka compares the architecture and design practiced at NBBJ with that of storytelling. Projects are infused with themes, values, ideas, images, metaphors, and vocabulary, all expressed in a finely crafted manner to enrich a community, an individual, and an author. "The spaces we design," she says, "should bring us to a consciousness of design that is immediate, that is beyond style and is about our times."

Her concern with design as an expression of our time explains an enthusiasm for the components of contemporary culture. Eminently stylish herself, she is fascinated with fashion, art, and music. Without awareness of these related arts, she believes, architecture and interiors cannot speak the language of your time. And conversely, "working with the arts," she says, "gives us a sense of the times outside architecture."

Her own Seattle residence, home for the past fifteen years, is one of effortless grace and comfort. With impeccable bones needing no architectural alteration, it is a serene environment filled with things collected by Suchecka and her architect husband. Furniture is celebrated for its object quality. Art and photographs abound.

Comfortable seating, a custom cocktail table, and vintage chaise create an inviting living room composition. The background color takes cues from surrounding greenery. Photos: Steve Keating

Old and new bentwood techniques come together in the dining room with vintage Thonet seating and Frank Gehry's contemporary icon. Arrangement of artworks complements the fenestration pattern. Photo: Steve Keating

In an era where pared-down modernism rules much of residential design, Kelly Wearstler's vibrant and densely layered interiors are a refreshing alternative. "I've never done a job with white walls. I always use a lot of color. Color comforts me," says the designer whose enthusiasm for the subject matches the exuberance of her own personality. Exotic elements are another hallmark of Wearstler's design. She mixes Asian artifacts, quirky flea-market finds, and fine antiques with pieces of her own design. The resulting compositions are testimony to her unerring eye and varied background. Educated at the Massachusetts College of Art and New York's School of Visual Arts, Wearstler apprenticed with Milton Glazer in New York and Cambridge Seven & Associates. Early on, she gained exposure to both large-scale architectural projects and graphics as they relate to all aspects of design.

With this solid training, Wearstler moved to Los Angeles, setting her sights on the film industry and production design. She distinguished herself from legions of Hollywood hopefuls by easily breaking into a notoriously tough business. But she realized the gypsy lifestyle and tunnel vision of production design weren't for her. Wearstler's daring and determined eclecticism required real people and sites plus a sense of permanence. Again, she didn't wait long for a professional breakthrough. Movie clients commissioned her for residential work; referrals led to a full-scale operation that has expanded to include hotel, office, and product design.

Wearstler's own apartment in the Hancock Park sector of Los Angeles best illustrates her offbeat approach. Each room has its own distinctive style and coloration. Yet a sense of harmony pervades thanks to the repeated use of vintage French and Asian elements, plus modern items designed by Wearstler herself. Almost every piece, says the designer, "has a wow factor."

In the living room, Wearstler's sofa and mirrored screen are modern complements to an Asian chair and antique French sconces. The focal artwork is a deconstructed Art Deco screen. Photos: Grey Crawford

(opposite) Treated like a salon, the dining room demonstrates Occidental and Oriental qualities with French antiques, a fretwork screen, and a silver-leafed lotus table base.

(below) A mural of stylized cherry blossoms shows Wearstler's interest in Asian motifs. Wicker chairs plus a custom-designed cane and wood television cabinet reinforce the theme. Photos: Grey Crawford

A Japanese screen headboard, silver-leaf table, bentwood ribbon chair, and magenta silk lounge chair are the main elements of Wearstler's bedroom. Vintage cards from Japanese cigarette packages are hung as framed art. Photos: Grey Crawford

"I used to be a hard-core modernist. SOM [Skidmore, Owings & Merrill] trained. Take me to the Knoll showroom and that was it. I was done shopping," Jeffry Weisman says. Twelve years in business have expanded his horizons. Not that the modern aesthetic and classic furnishings have lost their appeal; certain sites and clients demand them. But the challenge now, he says, is using all kinds of items to fit a project. "I don't find doing period rooms—whether they be old or new—very compelling." While developing the proper mix to suit both clients' personalities and their physical spaces is key to Weisman's approach, the designer cites another factor crucial to success. The element of scale is critical. "Scale," he says referring to any type of project, "makes it or breaks it."

Weisman completed undergraduate design training at Stanford with Phi Beta Kappa honors. He continued at Stanford, earning a graduate degree and then teaching. "I'm the only decorator with an MBA," he says. "And clients love it." Aside from business acumen, his advanced studies were invaluable in helping build a professional practice. "So many of my clients come from classmates. I have a history with these people."

The designer, who works on both East and West Coasts, names two major influences in his life and work. A long association with the incomparable Charles Pfister helped Weisman hone design skills and appreciate fine French and English antiques. Years in Italy, first as a student and then later as a professional on business and vacation travel, left indelible marks on his cultural and aesthetic conscious. "I continue to travel," Weisman says. "It continues to open my eyes."

(above) Antique mirror panels in a faux bois framework and dark-stained floors form a clean backdrop in Jeffry Weisman's and Andrew Fisher's San Francisco apartment. Within this setting, classical furniture—Louis XVI armchairs and a reproduction of Elsa Schiaparelli's living room sofa—looks particularly fresh. A quartet of architectural drawings by Sir John Soane and a gouache by California artist Oliver Jackson are cleverly mounted on the mirror.
Photo: Paul Margolies

(opposite) A brilliant red dining room in a Pacific Palisades, California, residence was built to accommodate the client's heirloom rug. Weisman designed the walnut table. Photos: Tim Street-Porter

Renovating a Palo Alto, California, apartment, Weisman revived the best of modernism in keeping with the building's 1960s origins. An open floor plan links the living room and kitchen for ease in entertaining. The classic Pfister sofa, plus Barcelona pieces, are softened by a rare Japanese screen and John Dickinson's quirky side table. Photos: Tim Street-Porter

Despite the generous proportions of the living room in a Pacific Palisades residence, Weisman limited furnishings in favor of airiness. Upholstered slipper chairs introduce bursts of color to the otherwise cool, neutral palette. Photo: Tim Street-Porter

dianna wong

Dianna Wong's aim for each project, regardless of scale, is a balance between the classic and the modern. Within architectural frameworks based on simple geometry and minimal color are references to the best of twentieth-century decorative design. "The overall goal," she says, "is to create a great sense of space and, at the same time, a reassuring sense of comfort and psychological well-being."

Wong's eclectic background consists of geographical diversity and an equally broad range of schooling and design training. Born in Hong Kong, she spent her childhood years in Montana, was educated on the East Coast, and became a practicing professional in Los Angeles. Wong graduated from Harvard College with a degree in studio arts, then earned a master's of architecture degree from Harvard's Graduate School of Design where she studied with Richard Meier and Jorge Silvetti. She continued her education on a traveling fellowship in architecture at Cambridge University, delving into the decorative arts, Japonisme, and the evolution of modern design. As an architect and associate partner, she was affiliated with Johnson Fain Partners; she expanded her interior design training at Hirsch Bedner Associates.

Among the first projects completed by her studio is a Pacific Heights residence for young members of the San Francisco Museum of Modern Art's board of trustees. Work encompassed renovation of the 7,000-square-foot (630-square-meter) Beaux Arts–inspired structure plus a rear, three-story addition. Wong's solution centered on creating classically proportioned rooms—ridding them of extraneous details, anchoring each with a strong focal point, and raising ceilings to bring in light and views. Furnishings reflect an evolution of style. Beidermeier is mixed with Mackintosh; Noguchi is combined with Wong. All, in the end, serve to enhance a museum-quality collection of art.

(above) Within the three-story Pacific Heights addition, the breakfast room has a 12-foot-high (3.6-meter-high), leveled ceiling accentuated by three colors of paint and cove lighting. The painting, Baltic States, is by Barry Russakis.

(opposite) Sliding beveled-glass doors (out of camera view) lead to the living room where a comfortable mix of furnishings includes velvet upholstered seating, a Noguchi table, silk draperies, and a Tibetan rug. Wong's mahogany mantel was inspired by Josef Hoffmann; the fireplace is flanked by Ameson's Up Against It Now and an untitled work by Ross Bleckner. Photos: Mathew Millman

The newly built master suite, with views to San Francisco's Golden Gate Bridge, is luxurious with a leather-paneled wall, mahogany and stone fireplace, and articulated crown moldings. The painting above the custom, leather-upholstered bed is by New York artist Barry Rattof. Photos: Mathew Millman

sara zook designs

An interior designer and furniture designer whose collection, New Classics Creations, has national showroom distribution, Sara Zook first defines her role as that of an educator and facilitator. "No matter how sophisticated my clients are, it is my responsibility to educate them, to help them stretch," she says. "The only way to do this is by involving them in the design process." Zook stresses process over product.

Programming, the key to any successful project, is more than a fact-finding mission for the designer. In addition to determining individual tastes and preferences, she delves into the subtler aspects of design, exploring the moods and messages the project should convey. Information in hand, she then develops several schematic solutions, each of which meets requirements. This way, Zook offers choices and combinations of choices throughout the presentation process. With clients involved in decision making from day one, Zook has carefully designed an approach meant to minimize disappointments.

While much of her residential commissions are concentrated in Colorado, the designer's work reflects a wider sphere of influence. She mixes regional influences with fine antiques, architectural elements, or contemporary pieces in efforts to avoid the obvious. Travel, too, exerts an unending influence. The pattern of a stone wall in China, a woven fabric in Nepal, a photographic study made of molding details in the Louvre—these are among her cited sources of inspiration.

Zook designed an 8,500-square-foot (765-square-meter) private ranch in Aspen. Overlooking a trout pond in front, the log and tin-roofed porch wraps around three sides of the house for outdoor entertaining. Pine and wicker furniture provides lounge and dining areas. Within the front door, ironwork in an abstracted cowboy motif sets the appropriate tone. Photos: Phillip Nilsson

(above) With the incomparable slopes of Colorado's Snowmass as a backdrop, the master bedroom of a 5,000-square-foot (450-square-meter) residence is furnished with maple case goods and a white-washed log bed. The cream/ecru palette is enlivened with red suede accents.

(opposite) Seating vignette is part of a large room dedicated to entertaining with a pool table and expansive bar. Overscaled seating, heavy chenille, and a warm gold/red palette imply warmth in this setting within a 5,000-square-foot (450-square-meter) Denver residence.
Photos: Phillip Nilsson

directory

design and architecture firms

Barbara Barry
9526 Pico Boulevard
Los Angeles, California 90035
(310) 276-9977

Thomas M. Beeton, Inc.
723½ North La Cienega Boulevard
Los Angeles, California 90069
(310) 657-5600

Hagy Belzberg
Belzberg Architects
9615 Brighton Way
Beverly Hills, California 90210
(310) 271-3087

Brayton & Hughes
250 Sutter Street
San Francisco, California 94108
(415) 291-8100

Brukoff Design Associates
480 Gate Five Road
Sausalito, California 94965
(415) 332-6350

Carmen Nordsten Igonda Design
8900 Melrose Avenue
Los Angeles, California 90069
(310) 246-0993

James Cutler
135 Parfitt Way
Bainbridge Island, Washington 98110
(206) 842-4710

Orlando Diaz-Azcuy
Orlando Diaz-Azcuy Designs
45 Maiden Lane
San Francisco, California 94108
(415) 362-4500

Mark Dziewulski
2618 El Paso Lane
Sacramento, California 95821
(916) 971-8900

Steven Ehrlich
Steven Ehrlich Architects
10865 Washington Boulevard
Culver City, California 90232
(310) 838-9700

John Erickson
Erickson Designs
24443 Zermatt Lane
Valencia, California 91355
(310) 477-9972

Ronald Frink
Ronald Frink Associates
2439 West Silver Lake Drive
Los Angeles, California 90039
(323) 662-0400

J. Frank Fitzgibbons
Fitzgibbons Associates
4822 Glencairn Road
Los Angeles, California 90027
(323) 663-7579

Frank + Frisch
125 East Linden Avenue
Burbank, California 91502
(818) 557-1818

Giannetti Architects
12225 Dorothy Street
Los Angeles, California 90049
(310) 820-1329

Hedge Design Collective
8670 Washington Boulevard
Culver City, California 90232
(310) 559-3714

William Hefner
5820 Wilshire Boulevard
Los Angeles, California 90036
(323) 931-1365

David Hertz
Syndesis, Inc.
2908 Colorado Avenue
Santa Monica, California 90404
(310) 829-9932

Gary Hutton
Gary Hutton Design
2100 Bryant Street
San Francisco, California 94110
(415) 626-2180

Israel Callas Shortridge Associates
254 South Robertson Boulevard
Beverly Hills, California 90211
(310) 652-8087

Kanner Architects
10924 Le Conte Avenue
Los Angeles, California 90024
(310) 208-0028

Craig Leavitt and Stephen Weaver
Leavitt/Weaver, Inc.
451 Tully Road
Modesto, California 95350
(209) 521-5125

Morphosis
2041 Colorado Avenue
Santa Monica, California 90404
(310) 453-2247

Brian Alfred Murphy
BAM
150 West Channel Road
Santa Monica, California 90402
(310) 459-0955

Olson Sundberg Architects
108 First Avenue South
Seattle, Washington 98104
(206) 624-5670

Polly Osborne
Osborne Architects
1525 S. Sepulveda Boulevard
Los Angeles, California 90025
(310) 447-2855

Antoine Predock
300 12 Street NW
Albuquerque, New Mexico 87102
(505) 843-7390

Pugh + Scarpa
Bergamot Station
2525 Michigan Avenue
Santa Monica, California 90404
(310) 828-0226

Rios Associates
8008 West Third Street
Los Angeles, California 90048
(323) 852-6717

Rockefeller/Hricak Architects
4052 Del Rey Avenue
Venice, California 90292
(310) 823-4220

Seccombe Design Associates
77 De Boom
San Francisco, CA 94107
(415) 957-9882

Sienna Architecture
411 Southwest Sixth Avenue
Portland, Oregon 97204
(503) 227-5616

Slifer Designs
105 Edwards Village Boulevard
Edwards, Colorado 81632
(970) 926-8200

Alisa Smith
3055 St. George Street
Los Angeles, California 90027
(323) 665-2047

John Staff
2148-C Federal Avenue
Los Angeles, California 90025
(310) 477-9972

Lenny Steinberg
Lenny Steinberg Design Associates
2517 Ocean Front Walk
Venice, California
(310) 827-0842

Madeline Stuart
Madeline Stuart & Associates
630 South La Brea Avenue
Los Angeles, California 90036
(323) 935-3305

Rysia Suchecka
NBBJ
101 South Jackson Street
Seattle, Washington
(206) 223-5555

Kelly Wearstler
KWID
113½ N. La Brea Avenue
Los Angeles, California 90036
(323) 931-8061

Jeffry Weisman
545 Sansome Street
San Francisco, California 94111
(415) 398-5434

Dianna Wong
315 West 9th Street
Los Angeles, California 90015
(213) 612-0888

Sara Zook
Sara Zook Designs, Ltd.
2001-A Youngfield Street
Golden, Colorado 80401
(303) 237-4544

photographers

Tom Bonner
Tom Bonner Photography
1201 Abbot Kinney Boulevard
Venice, California 90291
(301) 396-7125

Barry Brukoff
Brukoff Design Associates, Inc.
480 Gate Five Road
Suite 310
Sausalito, California 94965
(415) 332-6350

Jackson Butler
Hedge Design Collaborative
8670 Washington Boulevard
Culver City, California 90232
(310) 559-3712

Eduardo Calderon
11000 Holms Point Drive
Kirkland, Washington 98034
(425) 823-8242

Benny Chan
Footworks
824 17th Street, #5
Santa Monica, California 90403
(310) 449-0026

Grey Crawford
Grey Crawford Photography
2924 Park Center Drive
Los Angeles, California 90068
(213) 413-4299

Keith Cronin
Keith Cronin Photography
1887 Crossmill Way
Sacramento, California 95833
(916) 929-0189

Mike Ferguson
Hedge Design Collaborative
8670 Washington Boulevard
Culver City, California 90232
(310) 559-3712

David Glomb
74040 El Lilito Dr.
Rancho Mirage, California 92270
(760) 340-4455

Art Gray
171 Pier Avenue
#272
Santa Monica, California 90405
(310) 450-2806

Art Grice
P.O. Box 452
Rolling Bay, Washington 98061
(206) 842-1294

John Hughel
120 NW 9th Avenue
Suite 215
Portland, Oregon 97209
(503) 222-3730

Timothy Hursley
The Arkansas Office, Inc.
1911 West Markam
Little Rock, Arkansas 72205
(501) 372-0040

Steve Keating
Steve Keating Photography
36603 33rd Avenue West
Seattle, Washington 98119
(206) 282-6506

John Edward Linden
4422 Via Marina
Suite 703
Marina Del Rey, California 90292
(310) 301-4023

David Duncan Livingston
1036 Erica Road
Mill Valley, California 94941
(415) 383-0898

Mark Lohman
Mark Lohman Photography
1021 S. Fairfax Avenue
Los Angeles, California 90010
(323) 933-3359

William Mackenzie-Smith
MacKenzie-Smith Photography + Film
4758 Forman Avenue, #14
Tohiga Lake, California 91602
(818) 980-8228

Paul Margolies
50 Harbor Oak Drive
Tiburon, CA 94920
(415) 435-2671

David O. Marlow
The Marlow Group, Inc.
421 ABC
Suite J
Aspen, Colorado 81611
(970) 925-8882

Matthew Millman
Matthew Millman Photography
3127 Eton Avenue
Berkeley, California 94705
(510) 459-9030

Phillip Nilsson
Phillip Nilsson
805 W. Pine Road
Durango, Colorado 81301
(800) 252-1077

Ira Nowinski
Ira Nowinski Photographer
10 Allen Court
San Rafael, California 94901
(412) 495-6865

Stephen Oxenbury
7111 Hillside Avenue
Los Angeles, California 90046
(323) 874-7413

Erhard Pfeiffer
Erhard Pfeiffer Photographers
12406 Venice Boulevard
Suite 270
Los Angeles, California 90066
(310) 462-0096

Marvin Rand
1310 Abbot Kinney Boulevard
Venice, California 90291
(310) 396-0441

Derek Rath
4044 Moore Street
Los Angeles, California 90066
(310) 305-1342

J. Scott Smith
J. Scott Smith Photography
711 Pier Avenue
Santa Monica, California 90405
(310) 392-1300

Tim Street-Porter
2074 Watsonia Terrace
Los Angeles, California 90068
(323) 874-4278

John Sutton
John Sutton Photography
8 Main Street
Point San Quentin, California 94964
(415) 258-8100

John Vaughan
Vaughan & Associates
5242 Reedley Way
Castro Valley, California 94546
(510) 583-8075

Alex Vertikoff
Alexander Vertikoff Photography
P.O. Box 2079
Aherns, New Mexico 87059
(506) 281-7489

Dominique Vorillon
Dominque Vorillon Photogrpahy
1636 Silverwood Terrace
Los Angeles, California 90026
(323) 660-5883

Paul Warchol
Paul Warchol Photography
224 Centre Street
New York, New York
(212) 431-3461

Alan Weintraub
Alan Weintraub Photography
1823A Mason Street
San Francisco, California
(415) 553-8191

Joshua White
3008 Sentney Avenue
Culver City, California
(310) 202-6584

Toshi Yoshimi
Toshi Yoshimi Photography
4030 Camero Avenue
Los Angeles, California 90027
(323) 660-9043

Kim Zwarts
Atelier Kim Zwarts
Hertogoingel 29A
6211 NC Maastricht
Netherlands
00-31-43-3250761

For Viv and Len.

In 1993, I moved to Los Angeles. Except for my college roommate, I knew no one. Not a single designer, architect, or photographer. The grace and ease with which this community welcomed me was extraordinary. Now, working on this fast-track project, I am again overwhelmed by these professionals who have so generously cooperated. I look upon this as a collaborative venture, and offer heartfelt thanks to all participants.

Thanks, too, go to Alan and Lucas. They saw little of their wife and mother during this project's duration.

Finally, thanks to Nora Greer for her attention and support.

Edie Cohen, a long-time senior editor of Interior Design *magazine, moved to Los Angeles in 1993 to establish the magazine's first West Coast editorial office, where she writes about design projects there. She graduated cum laude from Syracuse University's Newhouse School of Journalism and also studied in Florence, Italy. Ms. Cohen resides in Santa Monica, California.*